D0590742

UAR

Please renew or return items by the date shown on your receipt

www.hertsdirect.org/libraries

Renewals and enquiries: 0300 123 4049

Textphone for hearing or speech impaired   0300 123 4041

Hertfordshire

521 258 63 0

www.BretwaldaBooks.com
@Bretwaldabooks
bretwaldabooks.blogspot.co.uk/
Bretwalda Books on Facebook

First Published 2014
Text Copyright © Bretewalda Books 2014
Cover design by dkb creative www.dkbcreative.com/
Gareth Jones asserts his moral rights to be regarded as the author of this book.
Bretwalda Books
Unit 8, Fir Tree Close, Epsom,
Surrey KT17 3LD
info@BretwaldaBooks.com
www.BretwaldaBooks.com
ISBN 978-1-909698-98-7

Printed and bound in Great Britain by
Marston Book Services Limited, Oxfordshire

Contents

Chapter 1:
Raining in the Rhineland

Tony Mealings is the one I have to blame for all those hours on coaches and thankless patrols of darkened hotel corridors in the early hours trying to get over excited young travellers to sleep when they are convinced they are on an eight day sleep over.

He is also to be thanked for getting me started on travelling with children and sharing with me the leadership of many of the European Tours.

The Rhine in Flood

Tony was Head of Music and I was Head of Drama at the school at which I still work.

These were innocent times in England. The first major theme parks had yet to be conceived and seaside fun fairs were still exciting. A swimming pool with a slide was an event and foreign holidays for families far less common. Tony and I had often travelled together and we decided that the children would enjoy the sort of holiday mix that we ourselves enjoyed, and so the Rhine Trip was planned, rolled out, and quickly populated.

The plan was to travel by coach to Dover, get the boat to Calais whilst enjoying a leisurely lunch, and then make the short journey to the Rhine Valley and our hotel in St Goarshausen, a small town on the banks of the river well placed for a mix of culture and fun. It didn't start well.

The flooded streets of St Goarshausen

We were aware before we left of the possibility of a strike by French Ferry workers over the busiest weekend of the schools' travel year, but we were advised to go anyway, and so we did.

When we got to Dover though it was clear that there was a problem as line after line of coaches clogged up the docks carrying what must have been thousands of children. The terminals were heaving with queues of ridiculous lengths and when we finally got to a desk to ask, hopefully, if we had time to let the kids off the coach for a break the helpful attendant replied that we did, because delays were currently running at 36 hours....Given that we lived two hours from the port this presented us with obvious choices, except that the only chance we had of crossing the channel was to hold our place in the queue, so we put on a film, VHS of course, and rang the company.

They were excellent and the boss actually turned up in his black BMW to operate a mobile office and provide support and cash to his trapped customers, whilst all the while trying to solve the problem, and solve it he did.

They must have had a dozen coaches on the docks but he managed to arrange tickets for all of his clients to cross as foot passengers on a Belgian ferry heading for Ostend, where a fleet of Belgian coaches that would take us to our various destinations would meet us. My abiding memory of that crossing is the kids stacked in the luggage racks because the ship was so full there were no other options, but in stoic British fashion we made the best of it and counted our blessings that a possible thirty six hours on the docks at Dover was, in the end, only eight.

After a bouncy crossing we disembarked, lugging our oversized luggage and carrying that belonging to the smaller children, to hopefully connect with a coach. The company was exceptionally well prepared and all the coaches were already clearly labelled, warm, dry and ready to go. We had not yet learned to travel with at least one full sized pillow whilst wearing loose clothing and with our shoes off, so we spent an uncomfortable journey through the endless rain to the outskirts of the Rhine.

Our first attempt to descend in to the valley was met with a black stream of water washing across the road. Our second attempt fared no better but on the third we actually managed to get in to St Goarshausen and sort of close to our hotel. Fortunately this was situated on the edge of the flooded streets, which, further down, were only accessible, by a network of connecting planks that stretched off in to the darkness.

Undeterred, and with no real choices we waded in to reception. The locals seemed quite used to this and completely un-phased so why should we worry?

With the party duly checked in we headed for a late meal, ankle deep in the swirling waters having a bit more of an adventure than we had banked on, the banks being the problem.

Once we had settled in we were determined to make the most of our first travelling adventure with children and so, the next day, we set off for PhantasiaLand, a theme park beyond the wildest dreams of all of us, but particularly of children from a small market town in rural Sussex. I do enjoy adrenalin driven experiences and have, on and off, both sky dived and been taken through extreme gliding {try a triple shandel if you're looking for a heightened moment} but there was a ride here that really scared me and made me wish I hadn't. I honestly can't remember its name but it was a combination of a detonator {taken to a ridiculous height and dropped}, a carousel {spun round till you feel sick} and a turbo helter-skelter {seemingly uncontrolled descent onto a hard mat}.

The problem was that I was young and not able to resist the peer pressure {"come on Sir, we will if you will, you know you want to, don't be a wimp!" and so forth} so I got on it. There was only a waist strap so how bad could it be? Very, was the answer, as I was about to find out.

Seat belted in to a small open rocket the ride began with a slow ascent to the top of an unfeasibly high pole, so far so good, but then it began to spin and then the rockets began to tilt and soon we were parallel with the ground and travelling at speed. The cocky kids had gone quiet and I was not happy but thinking I could cope. Then it began to descend at considerable speed towards the distant ground and we all began to "shout" in "exhilaration". Seconds later we wobbled off the bottom and began to convince each other that that was fun.....I haven't been on a ride of that type from that day to this and I never will, having become immune to peer pressure, I hope.

On other days we drifted up and down the now, slightly less awash gorge, by coach and boat and took the children and ourselves to a number of fascinating destinations. At one point we were all standing on top of the Lorelei, a four hundred foot rock from which the eponymous Siren, having committed suicide over a lost love, was famously want to lure boatmen to their death on the rocks below with the beauty of her singing.

Later we visited Rudesheim, a town actually designed to appear on a chocolate box {well it should have been} where we were entertained by Tony playing a piano once played by Liszt, or so we were told, in Siegfried's Mechanical Music Cabinet Museum. A building containing the most marvellous collection of weird and wonderful musical instruments, many powered by steam and all of which seemed to work.

We took the chairlift up to the Neiderswald to view the immense monument celebrating German Unification and went to Boppard for an encounter with Eagles and Owls and other elegant and dangerous birds of prey.

On one of these days I bought a set of Mosel glasses which, at the time I quite liked, leading the way for a frenzy of tourist shopping. How many of these still survive in cupboards round the town? Mine were given to my mother that Christmas, the following Christmas, neatly re-wrapped, they were given back to me....

One last day spent mostly in the wave pool at Cochem, which then seemed exotic and elaborate with its random water spurts and twisting tubes, and it was back to Calais for the short hop home.

Our first journey successfully completed and all of us bitten by the travelling bug.

Next year, Venice.

Chapter 2 - The Italian Jobs

Northern Italy and Northern Spain were our alternate destinations every Easter for almost two decades.

I first encountered Venice when I was back packing in the late seventies. Then I approached by rail over the causeway from Mestre arriving at the Santa Lucia station, a slightly incongruous but quite elegant Modernist building that fronts on to the Grand Canal.

This was in the days before you had to prove where you were staying before you could leave the station and I wandered through the meandering alley ways and tiny squares to the Rialto where, for the first time, I wondered at the view from the centre of the bridge up the Grand Canal which I have since taken hundreds of children to see. It really must be one of the great views of the urban world. {Randomly, I've just searched for a web cam and found a live feed scanning the Rialto but not, sadly, showing the view from the bridge.}

San Giorgio, Venice, taken on the move with 43 kids in tow

Wandering on I came into the great open space of St Marco and, for the only visit ever, found myself alone in the early morning light. I sat on the base of one of the pillars facing the amazing Basilica, as the sun began to pick up the ornate decoration of the five domes, just enjoying being there. {It became one of my standard answers over many years when asked by kids what there was to do to reply, "You don't need to do anything, just be here." I used this first to a boy who was comparing the Piazza unfavourably with the market square in his small Sussex town.} After a few moments a vehicle appeared, I've no idea where from, and began to hose the square down, causing me to move swiftly on to the water front and another amazing view down the Grand Canal to the right and across to San Giorgio.

This was years before I even thought of becoming a teacher, but when I did this was definitely a place we had to bring our students. Even the journey to it has produced a stream of memorable moments. With the flat lands of northern France crossed yet again, we generally head through Switzerland. This is always a nighttime experience shared with the children who have managed to stay awake to see the moonlit snow capped Alps either side. I recall a group of girls playing the "can I hold my breath through the tunnel?" game. They were doing quite well until in the hours before dawn they tried it with one tunnel to many. Blue faced and gasping they gave up one by one; it was the Great Saint Bernard, five thousand, seven hundred and ninety eight metres long and definitely a breath too far.

After the tunnel the road descends towards Italy and the stunning views of Lakes Lugano and Como, adorned with the villas and yachts of the super rich, and then it's down into the valley of the Po for the last long haul.

On one occasion I was passing this time by playing cards with some of the kids. They asked me how Poker worked and I taught them the simple game of five-card stud. On the first deal of the first game I dealt one boy his first ever hand. After a stunned pause from me he asked me if his hand was any good. It was. A royal straight flush in spades. Six hundred and forty nine thousand, seven hundred and thirty nine thousand to one against and the only time I've ever seen one in that game….for matches, on a coach, with kids.

We only ever stayed in Venice itself once, partly because the Hotels were just too expensive but also because the environs and activities just aren't child friendly. On the occasion that we did stay near St Marco some of the children found themselves in attic rooms with holes in the plaster and the party was split across two buildings with a canal and a rickety bridge in between. Far from ideal for them, but great for a colleague who ended up in a suite, with a view of Gondolas floating gently by. He did though eventually complain about the constant renditions of THAT song.

Our resort of choice therefore became Lido de Jesolo with its spacious streets, sandy beaches fronting on to the Adriatic and hundreds of Hotels. Whenever possible we chose the smaller ones where we were the only group because this made life so much easier. You get better at things as the trips pile up and in the early years of the Italian trip we did make the occasional mistake, like letting the children go out of the hotel, in groups of course and in a defined area, without realising that at fourteen they could legally hire mopeds to ride around the town, and so they did. I'll never forget the look on my colleagues' faces, and presumably on my own, as they spluttered in their coffee, when a group of boys came roaring {if a moped can roar} around a corner in full flight and blissfully free of crash helmets and any knowledge of the rules of the road. Thankfully they appeared later, unscathed, and were subsequently confused about why we thought this might have been a bad idea.

Venice itself has produced many memorable moments over the years so here are some in no particular chronological order.

There is always at least one child, and often several, who like the security of being around teachers and that's always been fine. It gives us a reason to use our days well rather than just drift around waiting for the kids. The only slight issue is lunch which they want cheaply and on the move and which we regard as the centre piece of any travelling day. In most places a pleasant meal in a high visibility restaurant can usually be achieved and the solution obviously is to take them with us and buy them a meal, which we have always been happy to do.

One child one year hit a sort of jackpot when he and I found ourselves sitting on a pleasant terrace at the right time. The alarm bells should have rung when the menu had no prices and the waiter offered to extend or withdraw our personal sunshades depending on our individual taste.

Partly because I like it and partly because I wanted to widen my companion's experience of food I ordered octopus fully expecting the usual plate of the little fried variety. What actually came out individually, were two large octopi sitting in a bed of rice, tentacles neatly rolled back, black eyes above a little beak staring balefully at us.

I've always had a travelling rule that I will eat whatever comes out if I order in a foreign language and something I wasn't expecting appears. This has produced some challenging moments but I've only failed once, in the Andes, an incident recorded elsewhere, and then I managed a nibble.

We stared at our food as it stared at us and then bravely cut in to the head, allowing a grayish mush to emerge, which we both momentarily assumed to be the brains and recoiled from our lunch. I steadied myself and tentatively took a small fork full and put it in my mouth expecting goodness knows what. It was asparagus and we both thoroughly enjoyed it.

The main course was an excellent lamb dish and the bill, well it was what you might expect sitting on the terrace of the Opera House.

Venice has always produced the most spectacular bills, along with some of the most spectacular meals. Try sitting on the Grand Canal with a lovely view of the Rialto and accepting the waiter's kind offer of a plate of the fish of the day if you have fire proof credit cards, or even better, stop for a drink in St Marks Square.

The cafes there are world famous and the haunts over the years of the great, the good and the great but not so good. With the sun shining and the orchestra playing you just have to sit in the sunshine or the shade {choose your side of the piazza} and take in the cosmopolitan atmosphere and the remarkable vista whilst sipping a cold drink in good company. The most I've ever paid there was seven pounds for a small bottle of Heineken in the context of a sixty pound round of lemonades and coffees {you do though get free nuts.}

One year two Australian back packers who were sitting at the next table amused us. They had clearly been there for some time if the number of bottles was anything to go by. As I paid our bill their eyes widened and when the waiter had left they leant over and asked if we had paid for just two drinks. When I said yes and explained that the price also goes up if the band play, they exchanged glances, picked up their packs surreptitiously and just ran. This must have become a regular event because in recent years, when we sit down, the waiters always show us the menu and point out the price, or perhaps with school kids in tow we just look cheap…The only time it topped that, and we didn't pay it, was when the US fleet turned up and the square was suddenly full of huge marines from the huge ships that filled the lagoon. The prices were suddenly inflated to match their pumped up muscles!

I never cease to be impressed by the impact that Venice has on young people. The sense of history and depth of culture is overwhelming and there are many "must dos".

One of the major advantages of staying at Lido de Jesolo is the journey in to Venice itself. The commercial ferry from Punta Sabbioni is a great experience. This bustling local service is cheap and regular and much better value than the private cruisers who will try to sell you their packages as you walk towards the pier.

Once loaded, the boats set off across the lagoon, pausing briefly at the smart and fashionable Lido de Venezia, before making the final crossing to its designated dock just down from the Doges Palace, the opening to St Marks and the impressive entrance to the Grand Canal. It is without doubt the only way to approach Venice, certainly for the first time.

Once ashore we always headed first in to the Palace itself. Pre-booking saves long queues and we were soon following the tour, building the kids up for the spectacular moment when we entered the Chamber of the Great Council which, at fifty three metres long and twenty five metres wide is at least half the size of a football pitch, with each and every metre of the walls and ceiling adorned with works by the great Venetian masters.

From there it's down a narrow twisting corridor and over the Bridge of Sighs, where prisoners got their last view of the outside world before descending to the dank, dark dungeons of the Piombi prison which once, famously, held Casanova.

Leaving that behind, the next highlight is the Campanile which, at ninety eight point six metres, dominates the city and provides stunning views, particularly over the roofs of St Marco itself, which is our next stop. Simply Magnificent.

A winding walk later and we are at the Rialto. The children always marvelled at my ability to deftly negotiate the winding back ways and narrow canal bridges, until I point up at the yellow signs with clear arrows that are everywhere.

Photos taken from the centre of the bridge, it's time for the safe and contained Rialto market where you can shop at either end of the scale. My house and many others in our town are full of chess sets, Backgammon sets, silly hats and little glass horses, with or without legs, bought just there.

This used to be a great place to haggle but as the years have gone by that seems to be less and less the case. We always try to teach the children a phrase or two and there and then it was "Troppo Caro" meaning "too expensive" which often came out as "Tropicana" causing much chaos, confusion and amusement.

The children were often far better at this than we were and we quickly learnt that sending a child to haggle with the Gondoliers often produced the best result and so they were all able to enjoy that iconic experience.

After lunch it's time for a challenge and we sent them off in groups to explore the many squares and churches and to find their own way back to San Marco for a glass blowing demonstration, always free, and a last bit of shopping in the inevitable shop that you are ushered in to afterwards.

Venice is all about islands and the larger ones, further out in the lagoon, can all be reached on the local waterbuses, after a stopping cruise down the Grand Canal and its period painted Palaces and a short walk to Fondamenta Nuovo. If time allows it's definitely worth diverting in to the Ghetto and having a look at the condensed floors where pressure of population made the Jewish community put seven storeys in to buildings where elsewhere in Venice they would have had only five. Shylock still haunts these atmospheric streets for those who know the tale of The Merchant of Venice.

Murano was the first stop at which we get off, the actual first stop being the impressive cemetery. Murano is famous for its glass manufacture and a good place to have lunch. Its picturesque main canal is always popular. A few years ago some of the girls in our group asked me to help them buy some glass gifts for their discerning parents. Happy to help, my wife and I took them in to a galleria where we had shopped in previous years. The owner was happy to take us upstairs to view his more extensive collection after my wife and I failed to agree on a piece to buy for our collection.

Half an hour later the girls had spent fifty pounds between them, we had spent a little short of five thousand and our colleague, who had laughed at our naivety, a mere three.... Thankfully our purchases proved to be good investments from which the grand children will benefit.

One more short hop and we were on Burano, the fishing island famous for its lace making. On the main street the houses are painted different colours, all in pastel shades. One story says that they are decorated thus to help fisherman find their way home in the deep mists that sometimes settle on the lagoon, others that the reason they need them picked out so is not the mist but the local grappa. Whatever the reason, it does make for a beautiful visit in the spring sunshine.

Torcello is the last of the big three. Populated after the fall of the Roman Empire when the land dwelling locals took refuge in the islands of the lagoon, it has a remarkable twelfth century Byzantine mosaic of the last supper on one of the walls in the largely seventh century cathedral.

We used to make the mistake of going back in to Venice until some bright child with a better sense of direction than us pointed out that we had in fact almost completed a full circle and that it would be much shorter to go on and complete the circular route back to Punta Sabbioni, or even better arrange for the coach to meet us at Treporti, even closer to the resort and therefore an even smarter move. Hmm.

Having tasted the delights of the city, in which you could spend years and still be discovering hidden treasures, it was always time to make the most of the area and head out on the coach for a series of visits.

The medieval heart of Treviso, with its excellent market, was the scene for an amusing farce one year. It is common for a student or two to be late for a check in but on this famous occasion the only person who made it back was the party leader, which wasn't me. He sat on the steps of the monumental and very hard-to-miss town hall and waited, and waited and waited some more. In the days before mobile phones there was little else that he could do. The rest of us, in four groups of around twelve, were all hopelessly lost having missed one key fact. We were trying to find our way by following a small canal without realizing that there were in fact several which curved and interlinked in a very confusing way. A camera in the sky would have tracked us missing each other by moments and almost getting out before mistakenly turning back, having decided we were definitely going the wrong way. To make things worse, when we finally emerged, embarrassed and confused, we had actually managed to really lose three boys who, it later transpired, had dived into a sweet shop convinced that they had time to stock up and catch up. They didn't. Our leader, now unusually cross, decided that we shouldn't split up and search since we would all almost certainly get lost again and so he called the police. They were very helpful and took him on a tour of Treviso in their squad car whilst others, with the photos we always carried, widened the search. They were eventually found sitting eating their sweets having done exactly what we always advise the kids to do in these circumstances which is to go and wait at the last place they saw a teacher, outside the sweet shop. At least they would never starve…

Verona is an easy journey away. This beautiful and elegant city centres on the lovely and fragrant Piazza della Erbe and the sleepy squares around it. One of these is the location of "Juliet's Balcony" in the house of the Capulet family. The entrance is always packed with fans waiting for their girlfriend to reach the front of the queue; sadly while they are waiting they seem to feel the need to declare their love by covering the walls in graffiti, a European habit that I've never been comfortable with. Just round the corner, past the raised stone tombs of the Scaligeri family, the house of Romeo is to be found, indicated only by a small plaque. Nice to think that they lived in such close proximity.

Another day we headed over the adjacent border in to what was then Yugoslavia. There were three target destinations each fascinating in their own ways.

The first was the caves at Postojna. An incredible complex of limestone caverns and formations that stretches for miles through the Karst of Slovenia.

The caves have been a celebrated tourist destination since the visit of Archduke Ferdinand the First in 1819 and the grand approach reflects that. Nothing though can prepare you for the caves themselves. Just to get in we had to load the group in to an opened topped Doto train that whizzes off through a series of low twisting tunnels deep in to the heart of the rock, with occasional wider sections giving a taste of what is to come. After ten minutes or so of thrilling turns where you do believe the instruction to keep your hands inside the carriage is actually important, you arrive at the station under the rock, disembark and walk into the first immense cavern. All tours are guided in the appropriate language and your first task is to get in the right group. Then you begin to climb the wet concrete paths into the lamp lit immensity of this first cathedral sized hall. This is truly a journey to the centre of the earth, or so it seems, with stalactites and mites on a giant scale all around you. Crossing bridges built by prisoners of war and passing areas of damage from exploded arsenals, you make your reverent way through the kilometres of accessible caves, many with a hint of even more endless tunnels beyond. A moment of truth arrives when they turn off all the lights. I've never experienced darkness like it. A blackness so complete that you could actually touch your eye and see nothing at all. Inevitably the moment is punctuated by excited squeals as the children scare each other with a sharp jab in the back.

At the end of the tour there is a subterranean river, hinting at the forces that formed this colossal feature, and then you are in a hall so big that orchestral concerts with audiences of hundreds are held there. Next, of course, the shop, and then the swift ride out. The last part of the tour used to be a small pool with live examples of the pallid "olm", a sightless lizard that looks only part-formed that lives naturally deep in the darkness. The stuff of legend, they were thought to be baby dragons forced up to the surface by rising water in times of storm, and from the look of them, who knows?

After the caves, and lunch of course, it is a short ride to the Lipica Stud farm, the home of the World Famous Lippizaner stallions, which is a must-stop destination for the girls in particular. We often got negative comments from boys about visiting horses until they saw these magnificent steeds strolling in their pastures, or even better close up in their stables. It seems odd that these essentially Spanish horses are bred in Slovenia to perform in the Spanish Riding School which is in Vienna, until you realise that the stud was established in 1580 by the Hapsburg Archduke Charles and that the Hapsburgs at one point controlled most of Europe, including Spain.

Before the revolution it was easy to drop down to Opatija on the Adriatic coast for a last stop of the day, now though that means crossing the Slovenian / Croatian border which can take a while.

Opatija is a hidden gem, a favoured watering hole of the Hapsburgs it is littered with fine buildings of a bygone age, many of which are now hotels. The seafront is truly beautiful and last time we were there we all amused ourselves by waving to family and friends on the live web cam that covers the bay, another occasion when mobile phones were very useful.

During an earlier visit, when Yugoslavia still was, we took a large group out for lunch in one of the fine fish restaurants that over looked the bay. It was the only time in any of our lives that we have seen hyperinflation in action as the waiter scrubbed the prices off a chalkboard twice during the meal to post the new ones, and this wasn't because we were tourists.

On the way back over the border we were able to fill the coach with cheese and drinks and still have enough to tip the girl on the till what seemed, from her reaction, a huge amount of money.

Two years later we decided to base our trip in Opatija so that the children would get the benefit of the power of hard currencies. This involved an even longer coach journey through Austria but we thought it would be worthwhile, and mostly it was. We were booked in to a five star hotel and we all had excellent rooms. The hotel boasted fine facilities, excellent food and a casino, which quickly caught our attention.

In order for you to appreciate the irony of this tale I must go back a step. A few days before, on a planned evening off, Tony and I had been to the casino and I had won. The children knew this and asked me on the coach the following day, how much. In a moment of mischief I pulled out a roll of money and a competition ensued, which lasted all day, to work out how much it was. At the end I got on to the microphone and announced that I had won a four-figure sum, at which there were gasps. Two, seven, four, eight. "He's won thousands," they said, until I added that there was a decimal point after the seven making it twenty seven pounds and forty eight pence. The roll of money was their spending money. I wasn't popular.

Some days later we were free again and so we returned. As we went in they gave us each a free five-deutschmark chip to get us started. There was only one roulette wheel open and that was surrounded by a coach load of Italians. Unable to reach, because I'm short, I approached the idle croupiers at the next wheel and asked them if I could play there and they were happy to oblige. I placed my chip on thirteen black {this is my system} and watched the ball whizzing around until, low and behold, it landed on my number. A pile of chips duly appeared and, over come by excitement, I came out with the immortal line, "Let it ride". The wheel spun and bang, unbelievable but true, thirteen came in again. Any sane man would have stopped at this point and I did leave the table, but only to move to the blackjack. This was also closed so I asked, and they agreed, to open it if I played three boxes simultaneously {this is very unusual}. I agreed and began to play, badly but with astonishing luck and don't recall losing a single hand on any of the boxes through the entire shoe. By the end everyone in the casino was gathered around watching the remarkable display of inept good fortune and a French lady with a feather boa was draped across my shoulders. Having politely got rid of her, I cashed in and actually emptied the casino of hard currency {it wasn't that big a casino.}

Next day of course when the story began to circulate it was met with a blank refusal to believe it, which served me right. The children did though get a day cruising on the Adriatic on a large steamer for very little money. They put the price down to the excellent exchange rate, it was actually down to the wheel and the blackjack table.

Our longest excursion that year was meant to be to the Plitvice National Park to the south, an area of an astonishingly beautiful combination of lakes and forests. Sadly, on the news the night before, a gun battle was reported just there. It was March 1991 and The Croatian War of Independence had broken out. We cancelled our excursion using the excuse that the passes were blocked by snow and the next day, after consultation, relocated the party to Jesolo, it was to be more than a decade before we were able to return. This was a source of sadness for us, but minor in the context of the tragedy that was unfolding all over the former Yugoslavia.

When we had been to Venice many times we decided to widen the experience of the children by setting up two-centre tours. The first of these was to Venice and Rome and for once we were going to fly. Things didn't start well when one of the staff had to pull out at the very last minute. Very professionally they had arranged a suitable replacement but hadn't taken on board the issue of the names on the tickets. There ensued a "discussion" at the flight assistance desk with the children already onboard and the luggage loaded, except for one but more of that later. The lady was frankly unhelpful and didn't want to take in to account that this wasn't an individual passenger passing on a ticket but an essential change for the sake and safety of the children. The exchange became more and more tense, until I asked to talk to someone who could simply authorise the change, since she could not and was insisting that we pay again, in full, which I was not prepared to do, either with the trip money or my own. Eventually the manager was rung and the phone handed to me. We discussed the problem, again, and I asked if they would like to disembark the 30 plus children and their luggage or could they just reprint the ticket. The Lady decided to reprint the ticket, at a cost of thirty pounds, ridiculous! We then had to deal with the boy who had picked up his mother's passport that morning rather than his own and no one had checked until we did. More phone calls and tension later and his parents agreed that they would send the passport in a taxi and that their son could catch the next plane. He was fifteen and the airline was now being helpful, so that was what happened. I waited for him at Marco Polo and we enjoyed an interesting journey on local buses and boats to find a hotel to which I had never been. Anyway, with mission accomplished, the holiday could begin.

Three days later, after the usual excursions, we set off for Rome planning to break our journey in Florence for lunch and culture, both of which the Florentines do with great style. Strolling through the Duomo and on into the squares around the Uffizzi is always a pleasure, even when one of the children's wallets had to be retrieved by my colleague Tim from an "inquisitive" local child, who was curious about its contents. That's what we decided anyway as a crowd of dubious characters began to gather.

Between us we have many portraits by the excellent street artists and have enjoyed many a good lunch in the tratorias around the Ponte Vecchio, and then it was off to Rome and our cosy hotel, so cosy that we decided to use one of the rooms as the TV lounge for the group. It was here that I was asked to translate a movie from Italian to English and so I did, even though I don't speak any more than the most basic Italian, I just sort of made it up as I watched the movie and it seemed to work. I had everyone convinced, even the staff, some of whom will only now, as they read this, realise that I was creating an original work on the hoof. Sorry.

Rome provided an endless stream of wow moments: strolling through the Forum in the warm rain that really brought out the colours of the marble, even if it did make them very slippery; watching the children get up the courage to place their hand in the lionesque "Mouth of Truth" and answer a random question {most were convinced that the legend wasn't true but somewhere in there believing that it might just bite their hand off}; and stopping at McDonalds to use the dryers in the loo to dry their heads and feet. Thankfully this was before the days of blade dryers, excellent for the hands but useless for these wider functions.

Having dried off we headed for the Vatican museum and began our journey through the endless galleries of modest statues until we arrived at the Sistine Chapel where, inevitably, the children were mildly reprimanded for lying on the floor to fully appreciate the astonishing ceiling.

The Basilica of St Peter completed our tour with even the most atheistic student overwhelmed, in one way or another, by the sheer opulence of this immense space.

No visit to Rome would be complete without a visit to the Coliseum. "Gladiator" was still a recent release and we could visualise the amphitheatre in all its gory glory. We all learned that day that naval battles were staged there for the appreciation of the baying crowds. Another year we decided to base the second part of our Italian adventure near Pisa and so booked accommodation in Marina de Massa, a pleasant sea side resort on the west coast. We soon found ourselves in Pisa itself and were impressed by the whole complex of white marble buildings. It took a while to get the photographs of each child with their hands supporting the leaning tower, and to usher them past the blanket stalls of the street traders with their neatly laid out "Rolex" watches. Kids from our college are often very astute and one pointed out to me that these clearly weren't real because the second arm ticked, rather than swept. By now they were experts at haggling and often got the price down by ninety percent, as opposed to one adult tourist who just bought one at the full price....I'll leave you to decide on his nationality.

We have never actually managed to get any children up the Leaning Tower, on the one occasion that it was open my colleague went on a reconnoitre and risk-assessed it out of the plan.

At Pisa though, lunch was the real problem, it was just too nice, even though the children have consistently failed to find any restaurant selling a "Leaning Tower of Pizza". One particularly sunny year we were there with another school group, with my friend Tony Mealings amongst their staff, and I wasn't party leader. We were having lunch with some students in a pavement restaurant and were mid main course when the time to leave arrived. Confident of our travelling abilities with heavily staffed groups and up for an adventure, we decided to stay and finish our lunch and make our way back later, in time for dinner. The distance, after all, was only forty miles or so. I decided that the fun thing to do would be to go to Pisa airport and hire a small plane with a pilot and fly back. There was a small airfield next to the hotel and the idea of being there when the coach got back was appealing. Phone calls to parents to gain permission later and lunch completed we set off. We hadn't though factored in that this was Easter Sunday in Italy. Oops again. It quickly became apparent that there were neither planes for hire, nor indeed any flights at all. Even taxies were an issue so after some debate we headed for the railway station. Fortunately there were trains and, after the second attempt, we ended up on the right one. Confident now we relaxed as the olive groves and vineyards rolled by until we saw the sign for Marina de Massa and got off. Unfortunately it was the wrong Marina de Massa, which turned out to be a district as well as a town.

When we realized that we were several miles from the hotel with no possibility of a taxi and no more trains we did the only sensible thing, bought ice cream. We could have rung up and had the coach come for us but that would have been too easy and a bit embarrassing so, suitably refreshed, we decided to walk. It was a nice walk for the first mile or so and then we began to flake. Moving from shade to shade and convincing ourselves that we did recognise the next corner and we were almost there we managed our despair until finally we did "stroll nonchalantly" through the gates, hiding the pain in our feet behind fixed grins. Chris though, who was later to come to Alaska with me, was happy that he had now been part of a Mr. Jones adventure, having heard tales of so many.

Chapter 3 - Romanian Tales

I can't for the life of me think why any school travel specialist company in its right mind would offer school tours to Romania whilst Ceausescu was still very much in control and the secret police were terrorising the population, but one of them did and so, enticed by a visit to Transylvania and curious about life in a communist country behind the Iron Curtain, off we went with, of course, a coach load of children.

First impressions were a little worrying as Tony tried to lower his tray on the plane and it promptly fell off into his lap, and drops of moisture began to drip on our heads.

Some hours later, after a spectacular flight and alarming descent, we arrived in Bucharest where we had our first taste of the nature of the regime. The airport was clearly shared between Tarom's passenger service and the Romanian Military, with jets, helicopters and tanks lined up on both sides of the runway. One of the kids tried to take a photo, much to the irritation of a grumpy and heavily armed guard, one of many standing around in the terminal.

We duly loaded all of our luggage, and the kids, on to our coach, on which the driver was wearing a long black leather coat and a flat cap. He looked like a secret policeman and, so it turned out, he was exactly that. We also met Alex, our friendly English speaking tour guide, who gave us a fascinating insight in to life under one of the strictest surviving communist dictatorships. We became friends and he later told us of his plans to escape to the West, which involved opening a bank account with enough foreign currency to "buy" a western tourist visa, and then claim asylum. When we got back we sent him the money, which wasn't much in our terms. We hope he succeeded but we never found out.

The bustle of Bucharest surrounded us as we drove across the heavily redeveloped concrete city, fascinated by the bendy buses with huge gas tanks on the roof and passengers bulging out of the doors, past Ceausescu's immense Palace, which was, Alex told us, the world's largest and heaviest civilian building, prompting one of the kids to ask whether it was also the ugliest {a little smile from Alex and a scowl from our "non-English speaking" driver.}

Driving out of the city on the way to our first hotel which was someway to the North, we actually passed a gang of workers cutting the grass down the sides of the road with scythes, a mixed bunch in a drab uniform. Questions about them were met with a sudden loss of English.

Hours later we finally arrived at our destination, having skirted around large areas that were suspiciously off limits, and checked in to our hotel which was in the main square. It was a solid eastern European concrete and plate glass structure with a smoky bar on the ground floor and a large restaurant, popular with the locals. Basic, but comfortable enough for our needs.

We settled the kids in and then went together for a walk around the town that, again, seemed largely rebuilt after World War 2. The children wanted to shop so we took them into a super-market, the shelves of which were mostly empty except for collections of little wooden boxes and Backgammon sets that looked very familiar.

That evening the Hotel decided to put on some entertainment for us. This was a game which involved the children coming up one at a time, being blind folded and then steered towards a long rope strung between two columns with bags dangling from it. These contained the prizes. After two or three goes it became obvious that all the bags contained exactly the same small plastic toy and a couple of sweets. It was already clear though, from the state of the shops, that considerable effort had gone in to this on their behalf and so we all responded suitably, much to the delight of the senior Russian officers sitting at the front table. These officers later ordered the removal by crash helmet-clad security guards of a local who, apparently, had taken offence at our presence and was saying unpleasant things, in Romanian. Looking back I imagine that restaurant was an expensive special events venue for the locals who weren't too impressed at getting there to find forty chatty foreign children occupying half of it.

The following day we were getting ready to leave for a day trip around some local sites, escorted of course, when we discovered the Hotel Dollar shop. Here, to the children's delight, we found chocolate and Pepsi-Cola, amidst the expensive watches and fur coats. Alex explained that these shops were to be found in most of the large hotels and that they were so called because you could only shop in them if you had hard currency. Their clientele therefore consisted entirely of tourists, mainly from other eastern bloc countries, and members of the Communist Party, because ordinary people weren't allowed to have hard currency.

We left the hotel, followed by the curious stares of the local children, and began our visits. Four hours later we had visited, ironically, three closed monasteries and a picnic area with a view. Returning to the hotel we passed a donkey-drawn gypsy cart with a rounded roof, open at the back, revealing any number of small children happily lying in a pile of loose hay, and that was on the motorway, the cobbled motorway. Later we stopped at a village school so the children could use the loo. I think they went through a steep learning curve when they saw the line of holes in the floor in the booth-less toilet and the lines of simple desks in the single bare classroom.

When we got back we had a discussion with the kids about our impressions of the day and we decided to act in some small way. It was too late to put our plan into effect that day but our plan was made.

After an early night, for once, we checked out, said our goodbyes, and drove off into the mountains of Transylvania.

Transylvania is now a mountainous region of Northern Romania. Up until the end of World War One it had been mostly in Hungary but its Nationality was reassigned by the far less well known sister of the Treaty of Versailles, the Treaty of Trianon, which settled the war in the east, so now it was in Romania. A decision that predictably created border disputes and a sense of bitterness that still survives in the second decade of the twenty first century.

This remote area is rugged and forested and roamed by wolves and bears even when we were there in the mid eighties. The towns and villages were small, connected by winding roads through a wild landscape. The local people, who dressed mostly in traditional costumes, and we don't think that was just for our benefit, seemed very disconnected from the communism and concrete of Bucharest.

Earlier in our journey we had stopped for a loo break in a frozen covered wood and the boys, who were looking for a tree to provide some semblance of privacy, found some bear tracks in the snow. It was a very short toilet stop after that. When they met some caged bears in a sort of a zoo later on, where we stopped for our regular ethnic lunch, they were very glad that we would not allow them to go looking in the dense undergrowth for the owner of the paws that made those tracks!

That night we stood on the balcony of our hotel rooms in our thermals {not just our thermals} with icicles like stalactites above us and the balustrade completely encased in ice that looked as if it had been there for a very long time, watching the clouds rushing across the moon and the wolves {seriously} running through the woods beneath us, so the scene was very definitely set for the centre piece of our tour.

High in one of Transylvania's {that must be one of the most evocative place names in the world} twisting gorges is a lonely castle {at least it was then}, sitting on a promontory at the end of a rising switch back trail, its towers piercing the torn clouds that swirl around it. It proudly dominates the landscape and the boulder filled valley below, or at least it did then. This was indeed the infamous Bran Castle, one of the homes of Vlad Dracula, the "inspiration" for Bram Stoker's 1897 Gothic horror story "Dracula". A book so scary that when I read it, aged thirteen, I had to sit with my back to the wall in a well lit room with my fingers carefully not touching the face of the eponymous vampire on the cover, and this place was our destination the next day.

The following morning we boarded our rickety old coach and set off, first down into the valley to visit Brasov and there we decided to enact our plan. Brasov is a large city in the interior of Romania that was later to become famous as a centre of protest during the revolution that unseated Ceausescu and led to his death.

When we arrived there, hours later, we went in to the dollar shop in the hotel on the main square with a collection of cash and bought all the Pepsi they had, which meant a tall stack of cases full of the original bottles. Then, we all, as a group, carried the wooden cases out in to the square and piled them up and then began handing the bottles out to passing local children. Initially suspicious, at first they wouldn't take them, but after one or two brave souls drank deep, an ever-growing crowd of happy faces with outstretched hands eager to taste this, to them, almost mythical drink, soon surrounded us.

Some police turned up, armed of course, but did nothing {if we had known anything about the regime we might have acted very differently. I suppose they were desperate for the currency we had and so allowed us our decadent western ways, or perhaps they just approved.}

The keeper of the dollar shop also joined us, clearly happy with what we were doing but also keen to stop the bottles disappearing, since they also, were currency in this impoverished community.

With the Pepsi all gone the crowd dispersed and we returned to the comfort of our coach, ready for the next part of our adventure, the trip to Castle Bran.

We all felt good about the whole thing, wisely or not, and were very happy years later, to see the good people of Romania free of the grip of Ceausescu and his family.

As we left the city we began rising again into mountains to the south. A short and spectacular journey later, we arrived at the foot of the track that led up to the Castle.

Our first thought was that the people who had done the research for the then recent movie, Bram Stoker's Dracula, had done a really good job, their castle and location were spot on, including high windows over the gorge, ideal for defenestration, something for which this tyrant was apparently particularly well known.

What was less impressive was our first obstacle to entry, the, I suppose, inevitable line of stalls selling Dracula memorabilia. Mini Count Dracula's with red teeth, red teeth you could stick in your own mouth, little plastic castles and all the rest. I'm pretty sure that there must be a factory somewhere in Eastern Europe producing this "local handicraft", for the world, same rubbish, different mould. Does the Eiffel Tower machine sit alongside the Big Ben machine, which sits alongside the Parthenon Press? I wonder which is their biggest seller? Probably the "guaranteed to be locally hand-made by people who really need the money ethnic beads machine".

Anyway, we all shopped happily and I bought yet another

Backgammon board and then, after refreshing ourselves at the roadside stalls selling local pastries and something-flavoured drinks, we slowly began the climb.

At the gates of the castle we all sat down and I told them the story of the book and the story of the real man, having fended off the "official" guide with his handmade badge. I would normally let the guides have their moment but this particular man could only offer talks in Romanian, Russian or German, impressive in itself but of no use to we English who could muster at best, a smattering of French. It's important to set the scene for visits like this, otherwise all you are doing is wandering around yet another castle, but there is a definite art in balancing the drama with the age of the children and much of what Vlad Dracula had allegedly done, could not be repeated. If you want to know more about the activities of a man so cruel that his actions spawned the legend of the ultimate vampire monster, you must look elsewhere.

My recollection of our visit is of young explorers, with some trepidation, moving in small huddles around the dark and bare interiors, the bare rooms being adorned with little more than the occasional small oil painting of Vlad Dracula himself. Did those red eyes follow us as we moved from room to room? Or did those shadows coalesce as we wandered up and down the narrow stone stairwells that did not seem to conform to the rule that spiral staircases always turn the same way to inconvenience right-handed attackers?

My visit today, courtesy of the internet, shows a very different place. White washed hotel rooms in a built up area, so perhaps we saw it at its best.

Was that a bat that flew out of the woods as we made our way down the darkening slopes? The startled cry of one of the children makes me think it was. Over the years we've slept in all sorts of places as other pages in this book attest, but in Dracula's actual castle in the midst of snow clad mountains, I think not.

Chapter 4 - Storm at Sea

Back in the eighties there was a popular movement in favour of taking children on educational cruises. Our RE department decided to organise a party to join the MS Jupiter on a cruise of the Eastern Mediterranean and I, as a seasoned traveller in my own right and a qualified historian and archaeologist, was invited along as part of the team.

The itinerary looked fascinating: flying into Ataturk airport for a transfer to Istanbul docks to board our liner, followed by visits to Port Said and the Pyramids at Giza; a visit to Israel for Jerusalem; and then on to Kusadasi for the astonishing ruins at Ephesus; next was Rhodes, then Athens and the flight home.

This was a new venture for me and even newer for many of the kids, who had never flown before, let alone flown down to the Mediterranean for a leisurely cruise.

The bus transfer and boarding was uneventful but then we faced our first dilemma: with time before dinner and hours before we sailed, moored in the harbour of one of the world's most historic, significant and mysterious cities, what choice did we have? We had to get off the boat in the darkening evening light and go and explore, so accompanied by one of the ladies and several children we set off "bravely" in the direction of the famous Grand Bazaar. A market so old that its history stretched through Byzantium and almost back to Constantinople itself.

We actually did quite well, given my history of confidently leading groups off into a maze of streets actually convinced that I do know where I am going when, in fact, I really haven't a clue and I'm just relying on a general sense of direction.

We did talk about it first and decided that if we headed up hill from the port the Bazaar was so big that we really couldn't miss it. Oops!

We hadn't banked on the concealed nature of the entrances to this completely roofed and heavily disguised, massively complex web of streets and alleys and I reckon we walked around the outside at least twice before I had the good sense to actually ask. My enquiry in English failed but basic German did the trick and with a little smile the fez-wearing local pointed towards a cavernous entrance no more than twenty yards away.

So in we went and we were so glad that we had decided to have this adventure.

Research after the event revealed that we had just walked in to a five hundred year old "Kapalicarsi" or covered market made of sixty one streets and over three thousand shops.

The fading evening light still contributed something through the high windows and sky lights, but by now most illumination was being provided by oil lamps suspended above the open fronts of the fabulous shops which were selling a wonderful mix of goods; carpets {of course}, spices, leather, pottery, long flowing jellabas beautifully embroidered, sweetmeats and pastries and mint tea and, inevitably, Backgammon sets.

We strolled for a good hour amongst the throng, enjoying the babble of foreign tongues and the exotic sights and smells of this very alien place. Each shop we passed brought a friendly salutation from the vendors, one of whom looked remarkably like Sidney Greenstreet in Casablanca. He invited us in to his carpet shop and graciously and without agenda gave us mint tea. This was a first for me as well as the children, who all politely accepted his kindness and bravely sipped the scalding liquid.

The purchase of one Backgammon set later {he sold more than carpets} and with many handshakes and wishes for a long life and a happy future we went on in our exploration.

My recollection is that we spent a long time wandering but it cannot have been because eventually we got back in time for dinner. Dinner was made less urgent by our consumption of Turkish delight and baklava in the tiny open cafes that were dotted around.

Finally we decided to leave and made our way to the exit. We thought it was the exit that we had entered by, blissfully unaware of the sheer size of the Grand Bazaar. We had turned right to enter so exited and turned left. The road conveniently began to descend towards the shore and so our little crocodile, with me confidently in the lead, marched on in to the night in, of course, completely the wrong direction.

After a little while I realised that things were not going well. We walked into a spice market; an ancient covered street lined with sacks of brightly coloured pungent powders and found ourselves standing on one end of the Galata Bridge, which famously crosses the Golden Horn. I was actually secretly pleased because this was one of my targets and we had just stumbled upon it and I only wish we had had the time to take the kids down one of the rickety wooden staircases to sample the fare in its famous fish restaurants. I have returned a number of times since with family and friends and we really did miss out. Eating fish there whilst the sun sets is still one of my favourite food experiences.

The time though had definitely come to get back to the ship and so we set off along the shoreline. A young man emerged from the darkness and my defensive instincts bristled. As it turned out he was a student of English who had heard us chatting and praising that amazing city. He just wanted to talk and was very happy to accompany us back over the hill {wrong shoreline….} to our ship where we shook hands and said goodbye, ready for the next stage of our adventure.

Safely onboard and exhilarated by our experience we ate and rested as the ship edged its way out in to the busy lanes of the Bosporus and pointed its bow south towards the Mediterranean. As we sailed I regaled the party with tails of ancient Troy, the ruins of which were passing invisibly to our left, now far inland.

We had a good night's sleep but we woke to a very different motion. During the dark hours a wind had sprung up which was pushing the grey sea in long lateral waves in what seemed to be the most uncomfortable direction possible. We went on deck to explore at the front of the ship and were literally reduced to holding on to the railings round the deck to keep our feet. It only took a few moments to realise that we should be inside and so we went.

I had a hearty breakfast but most of our group, in fact most of all the groups, began to look increasingly green and unhappy and inevitably, like a chain reaction, passengers young and old began to feel sick. I've always been fortunate in this respect and so was able to busy myself trying to help others to feel more comfortable, directing our kids to the mid section of the ship and recommending a lower deck, since this was the place where the ship moved least.

It was a very long day. The thunder and lightning crashed and flashed around us as we rolled across the middle of the middle sea. The passengers, mostly under 16, were really not coping and the public loos quickly became places to avoid..........the restaurants though were empty apart from a few well-fed diehards. My luck though was not going to last.

The medical officer decided enough was enough and began to hand out free anti seasickness pills. At first I thought I wouldn't bother but then, giving in to peer pressure, I decided that it couldn't do any harm... so why not?

The "why not" was that, even though I didn't suffer from mal de mer I was clearly allergic to the pills meant to cure it and I almost immediately began to retch and then….well, you can imagine. We had all long since retired to our cabins and the comforts of our very small en-suites. Unfortunately there was only one loo and two people. My third colleague famously described the two of us as looking like a pair of those nodding birds dipping their beaks in a pond as we literally took it in turns to ease our discomfort.

Things were getting serious and the Captain decided that we should not attempt the approach to Alexandria, our intended port of call, because the conditions simply made it too dangerous, so we limped along the coast in slighter seas until we arrived safely at Port Said, the northern entrance of the Suez Canal.

So we missed looking for signs of the Lighthouse but were rewarded by the sight of the fleet of ships waiting to head down the waterway to the Red Sea. We loaded up on to a fleet of coaches and set off for Cairo, our targets being the Tutankhamen exhibition and, of course, the Great Pyramids at Giza.

We all enjoyed the ride across the desert into the green landscapes of the Valley of the Nile and experienced that classic view of the region, a huge tanker apparently sailing across the desert.

The cosmopolitan bustle of Cairo and the lazy winding of the Nile also impressed us. Unfortunately we were running late and the Museum wasn't able to stay open for us and so the treasures of the boy king would have to wait for another day {I've successfully missed them several times since} and so we headed straight for Giza.

In the eighties this was a strange place. Our minds were full of swelling dunes and swelling tunes and sunsets through the palms silhouetting this ancient wonder of the world, guarded by the brooding Sphinx. The reality was somewhat different.

The Royal Burial Site is right next to a particularly poor neighbourhood of Cairo. If you faced one way you did in fact have a fabulous view of the Pyramids and the desert, but if you turned around you were confronted with a particularly unsavoury collection of shabby buildings, litter and dogs, although I'm sure that it is much nicer now…..

The coach pulled up on a slope above the main site and we started to get off. This was our first mistake. Within seconds the various vendors, guides and Camel Guys had rode in to the group and split it in to three. Two girls were plonked on a donkey, which immediately began to leave and some other man was actually half carrying off one boy. We had to react quickly, one of my colleagues set off after the girls whilst I retrieved the boy, much to the surprise of the man who actually fell over. The other staff got the kids back on the bus and, all together again and safe, we blocked the door.

Unwilling to simply drive away we had to think of a plan and I decided that the best thing we could do would be to give our business to one of the bigger, older, tougher looking vendors and let him sort out the rest. This worked and soon we were able to get the kids off the coach and gather them on a safe piece of rising ground. From there we were able to enjoy, if enjoy is the word, the camel rides down to the Pyramid of Cheops, and explore the environs in relative safety. Not though without having to pretty much put a cordon around the kids to keep the endless stream of people wanting to sell them things or take them to see something on their own "for you a special price" guided tours.

I don't resent any of this, when you visit areas of great poverty with, for them, great wealth in your pocket, you expect to get a lot of attention, but for me at least it did spoil the day and, perhaps sadly, I've never been back to any part of Egypt again.

Another blow awaited us when we got back to the ship. There had been an outbreak of unrest in Israel and the decision had been made that it would be too dangerous to go there so Jerusalem would have to wait, and it still does. I did though get to see it with my wife from Mount Nebo in Jordan a few years ago.

Instead we were off to Rhodes and, as it turned out, a Big Fun Greek Wedding.

We had already missed out on any possibility of seeing the Pharos of Alexandria and had been deeply disappointed by the Pyramids so we were looking forward to at least being in the location of the next ancient wonder of the world, the Colossus of Rhodes. As we sailed in to Rhodes harbour I painted a word picture of the immense bronze statue of the Titan Helios, which actually never straddled the harbour mouth but, most likely, stood to one side. Completed around 280BC by Chares of Lindos, it fell during the earthquake of 226BC and was never restored. At 30 to 33 metres high it must indeed have been a wonder.

We landed early in the day and boarded our coaches for a short drive to the ruins of Kamiros, an ancient Hellenistic city long abandoned. The dramatic setting above the cliffs of the north west shore made the visit memorable, and whetted our appetite for the visit to Ephesus that still lay ahead of us.

We returned to Rhodes city for the afternoon and went for a wander in the old town and, as luck would have it, we found ourselves in a narrow winding street that seemed to have been completely taken over by a wedding party. Unsure whether we should pass through or go back and not wanting to cause any offence, we just stood. We were though soon noticed and invited in to the party, our hands were filled with candied almonds and, amidst much smiling and laughter we were soon all dancing around in the circles of revellers and having a great time. Even the retsina tasted good, perhaps it just doesn't travel well.

It was clear that the festivities were settling in for the duration and we had to go but that happy hour mixing with those friendly people and dancing, what I later discovered was a "Karlamantiano" was one of the highlights of the trip.

Soon Rhodes was behind us and we were heading for the Turkish mainland and the port of Kusadasi. Another successful docking later{we really enjoyed the manoeuvrings and often gave the Captain advice, if only amongst ourselves} we were ready for our visit to Ephesus.

We had been told that all the best Greek ruins were in Turkey. I'm not sure that is completely true but they certainly do have some excellent examples and Ephesus was definitely the best I've ever seen. Our next ancient wonder was here, The Temple of Artemis, the towering columns of which were still impressive, so we were off to a good start. It was actually raining at first but that didn't dampen our enjoyment, it actually helped by bringing the marbles to life and giving them a more vibrant sense of colour.

We stopped at the famous library before making our way to the immense amphitheatre. It was here that St Paul, according to some, had preached to the Ephesians and that made it a place of great interest, but we had also been told that the acoustics were well nigh perfect and that if you dropped a coin in the centre spot at the bottom, people in the top row at the back would be able to hear it. Inevitably, we had to try this out.

By now the sun was out and the place was busy with tourists. We sent off some of the fitter children to climb to the top and once they were nicely spread out I made the request, in my best drama teacher's voice. "Ladies and Gentlemen, could I have your attention please. We would like to test the theory that a coin dropped here will be heard at the top of the amphitheatre. Can I ask you all to be silent please and raise your hand if you hear the sound?" Everyone co-operated and the place was soon silent and still. Our designated coin dropper dropped the coin and the hands went up, like a Mexican wave, right to the top.

Mission accomplished and marked by a significant round of applause we returned to the ship ready to sail across the Aegean to Piraeus, the port of Athens, and our final destination.

I had been here before, in the late seventies, so knew that high on the list should be the Archaeological museum, the Acropolis and the Plaka district. In those days I was travelling as an almost penniless student and I had, and still have, fond memories of sitting in Monastiraki Square sipping a cold drink and listening to an itinerant band of laid back musicians playing Eagles numbers under a blazing sky, before strolling through the meandering streets of the Plaka district to climb the stone stairs to the Parthenon.

The buses took us along the long walls from Piraeus, past the spot from which the Piraeus Lion with its eleventh century Viking runes carved, presumably, by some warrior of the Varangian Guard, was looted. That now stands outside the Campo Arsenale in Venice, another target for a later trip.

A couple of hours later and we had achieved the fine museum and were heading for the Square through the eccentric traffic of central Athens. We spent the journey trying to work out the rules, and miserably failing as cars flew in all directions. It was some years later, on a family holiday, that I finally plucked up the nerve to hire a car and discovered what the rule for cross roads was when I was told by the Rep to "just close your eyes and go". It seemed to work….

Anyway, we eventually arrived safely and, lo and behold, the musicians were still there, at least it could have been them. We all settled down in a mix of sun and shade and enjoyed the music for a while before dropping our coins in their guitar cases and heading off.

The Plaka, like the rest of the now famous tourist stopovers, was still charming but very different. The streets were just as winding but the smoky bars and little local-owned cafes had been replaced by air conditioned eateries and tee shirt shops. So the kids bought tee shirts and I bought a Backgammon set, forgetting my own advice to always buy on the way back and at the end of the day.

What seemed like hundreds of steps later, and under a baking sun, we made it to the summit and were blown away by the breathtaking scale of this most famous survivor of ancient Greece. Years before I had sat amongst its columns to eat my lunch, now we had to be content with a view from behind a rope, but it did look cleaner and restoration work was clearly underway, so that was good.

One of the young explorers had recently been to the British Museum with her Dad and a discussion broke out over the Elgin Marbles. A fierce debate, worthy of the Athenians, later the majority view was that they wouldn't exist if Lord Elgin hadn't "salvaged" them from the blown up ruins so they were better off where they were. However there were many who took the opposing view, thanking Lord Elgin for his thoughtfulness but thinking that the British Government should now graciously return them to their natural home.

After a burst of team photo taking with everyone needing their own we set off again, but this time to pick up our luggage, say goodbye to the ship and head for the airport and our uneventful flight home.

Chapter 5 - All things Catalonian

Tarragona by Torchlight

Tarragona is an ancient city that has played host to many fascinating travelling tales. It has straddled the bay since long before Roman times, as evidenced by the massive square cut stones of the ancient walls. As Tarraconensis it was home to Augustus, Galba and Hadrian, and boasted fine palaces and villas. The thriving medieval town it developed into is still there, with twisting streets, a grand Cathedral and great sweet shops…

As with many of the places we took children, I first travelled there with friends and determined to return to its Amphitheatre, old town, Ramblas and restaurants.

Spain 2010. Dominic and Eric the Snowman in Tarragona having witnessed the Castells Competition

In recent years though Salou has sold its financial soul to the "Saloufest" at Easter, for which no blame should be attached. The offer of almost full occupancy and over flowing bars before the official start of the season cannot be easily turned away.

This is a University "Sports Tour" much featured in the British press, which seems to revolve around groups of very drunk students dressed in ridiculous fancy dress {twenty pink Emu's in tights, for example} behaving, in my view, in a way that creates an appalling image of British youth and makes the otherwise pleasant and attractive resort unusable by school groups during those weeks. I can't describe their behaviour in any more detail but I'm sure you can work it out.

Tarragona though, for children, is great. The beach, if you can sort sufficient life guards, is sandy and safe and the old town {Cuidad Medieval} north of the Rambla Vella, is enclosed by the walls of the ancient city.

It was though on the Rambla Nova that we introduced the children to tapas, in the form of "pulpitos", deep fried baby octopus, and "Granisadas de Limon", a wonderful drink of fresh lemon juice and crushed ice. A great way to divide the day, whilst sitting outside a pleasant café on the Balcony of the Ocean in the heat of the noon day sun.

Years ago this would have been followed by a scramble over the ruins of the Amphitheatre, an enjoyable activity which sadly, like so many, has been risk assessed out of existence, so nowadays we take the party for a stroll through the winding streets to the Cathedral and then divide our time between shopping and the beach.

The Cathedral once caused the children huge amusement when I tried to pay the small entry fee by asking for the tickets in passable Spanish, only to be cut short by the formidable lady at the desk who insisted on teaching me how to achieve this in Catalan. As a Welsh man I had a fighting chance at the pronunciation but it was very funny and very phlegmy and took a long time.

One of my targets has always been to watch the Catalan villagers competing in the building of the human towers. Called Castells these can be up to ten layers high, topped with a small boy who clambers up the outside once the structure is almost complete. I've seen many pictures and walked past many statues so, although pleased for the group, it did cause a sense of regret when some boys came back from their independent exploration with tales and photos of a large competition of just this which had just taken place in the next square along. "You couldn't ring me", I said, "Sorry" they said.

To rub it in they had been entrusted with our special guest, "Eric the Snowman" who is a regular intercontinental traveller with his own Facebook page and fan club and they had failed to get a photo of him on top of one of the competing Castells. Just too much to absorb, but a wonderful experience for them, and it just means I'll have to go back, with Eric, again. Oh well…

The main attraction though of Tarragona is the Easter Procession, something that we always took our young travelling companions to see.

On Good Friday the old town and the Ramblas are prepared. Temporary stands are erected and chairs line the streets and squares. In the churches and the Cathedral, giant floats are waiting, each depicting a different scene of the Calvary story in the procession of Santo Entierro. In the houses of the faithful in Tarragona and the villages that surround it, the three thousand or so participants are preparing their costumes and penitential garb.

As night falls, the crowds begin to gather and the stands and streets fill to bursting. I have no way of calculating how many but there is no spare room anywhere, it must be close to six figures and feels like many more, and into these narrow, twisting over-crowded streets we took our group of students……… only once though. The first time we made the mistake of getting there very early and waiting outside the Cathedral itself. As the evening unfolded it became clear that this was going to be a very long event and so we tried to quietly and respectfully make our way down the hill to leave, it took a while.

In other years though we got it right and waited on the Rambla Nova for the procession to come to us. Our largest group consisted of 137 students aged between twelve and sixteen. These were the days before mobile phones so we had to have quick and easy ways of checking them in. This year we had the bright idea of forming a human arch and counting them through one by one. The first problem was that I am not very tall and some of the children are, so I had to be replaced, and then the counting began, much to the amusement of some of the locals who probably count their goats or sheep in much the same way.

The first time we made it one hundred and thirty six, the next a hundred and thirty eight and finally a hundred and thirty seven…. so that was OK. {Now we divide parties in to groups based on their hotel rooms, allocate three rooms to a teacher and just call out, "check in". Within a minute groups of any size can be counted and the teacher's hand raised, to indicate that all are present and safe.}

All accounted for, we positioned the students along the downhill side of the road, so we could melt away without causing a disturbance, lined up the staff behind them to ward off any potential pick pockets, and waited.

The first thing you hear is the beating of the drums echoing around the antique walls, then around the corner comes a troop of Roman Legionaries in full ceremonial armour. Next come the drum corps, a mix of old and young but all male, and then the first of the religious floats. These are carried by, maybe, eighty men, about half of them visible, with the others actually underneath the iconic scene, with only their feet on show. As they lift the long poles that support the float the statues rock from side to side casting long shadows, lit as they are by the torches held by the hooded figures around them. Another section of the procession is made up of black clad penitents walking in bare feet and praying with their rosaries, and another of ornately regaled Priests and altar boys swinging their incense burners {technically called thuribles, I've just discovered}.

Any tourist foolish enough to make noise, which our children never have, are instantly told to hush by the devout Tarragonese, to whom this is clearly an event of great importance and significance.

It can take hours for the full procession to wind its way out of the old town so we have never seen the end. After an hour or so of exposure to this sort of faith and worship, the children are always quiet and thoughtful having had their first encounter, for most, with ancient traditions and profound unquestioning belief.

Montserrat and the cable car

It was just one of those moments when you've thought it so you have to say it.

We were visiting Montserrat, the astonishing monastery on a mountain inland from Barcelona.

The location itself an amazing thing, this huge mass of bare rock that soars up out of the hilly plains that really does look as if it has been sawn and planed into a series of pinnacles by some designing force. It is a unique feature that can be easily identified half an hour before you actually get there.

This wonderful place is a destination of choice on all of our Spanish trips for so many reasons, not just the spectacular geology, landscapes and views, but also the religious and cultural significance.

The monastery has been there since the 12th century and was founded after the discovery of the Black Madonna, many years before. This wooden statue, according to the local legend or story, was found in a cave on the mountain after a series of signs from God. It has been venerated here ever since and so Montserrat has become one of the great centres of pilgrimage of the Catholic Church.

Renowned also as a centre of learning, one of its abbots went on to become Pope Julius the Second, the great patron of Michelangelo, and also for the boys' choir, which we have been privileged to hear many times, and which is world famous.

Whenever we take children there we are always impressed by how many want to join the queue to touch the Black Madonna and light a candle, and also stand in respectful quiet as the choir sings in the great church, which actually was rebuilt after an attack by the French in 1812.

It's one of those places where you think the first level is high, which it is, but then you ride the funicular railways to the very top and you can see the French border in one direction and the Balearics in the other.

Definitely the best way to approach Montserrat is in, or is it on, the little yellow cable car. Fully enclosed and perfectly safe it carries about 40 people at a go, all scrunched in with no seating. OK, so it sways a bit and rushes across ravines and rock faces in quite an alarming way but we all know it's perfectly safe, making the journey up and down the mountain all day everyday as long as there are people who want to be carried to the main level, and it isn't lunch time.

Each time that we have been there we have stopped the coach and given the children time to get off and take in just how high this cable car is. The car itself looks small at the bottom but by the time it has swung out over the stomach dropping heights it is the merest dot. Every year there are some young travellers who simple can't get on it, and that's fine. They are carried to the main level in the coach up the twisting mountain road with the curtains drawn seated in the middle. This always means a teacher has to go that way too, but there is usually someone only too happy to volunteer and, if not, it's me.

My friend Nicky, who was helping out by coming along as staff with a particularly large group, was to blame really because she asked me a provocative question, and I was prone to giving in to temptation when these opportunities present themselves.

"What would happen if the cable broke half way up?" says Nicky, her question being overheard by many of the children.

Well, the answer clearly would be that everyone would die but I couldn't say that because half the kids would refuse to get on so instead I got on to the coach's microphone and made the following announcement:

"Some concerns have been expressed by the staff about the safety of the cable car so I'm pleased to be able to tell you that, fortunately for us, NASA chose this place last year as a testing ground for a new propulsion unit which they claim is a prototype for a safety system. As a result they installed mini jets in the base of the cable cars so that if the wire does snap, or the car just falls off, the computerised guidance system will lower it gently to the ground."

There was a long moment when glances were exchanged by staff and children, all of whom were clearly weighing up whether or not this was actually true and hoping that it was.

Nicky, to be fair, twigged almost fast enough to avoid too much embarrassment but many of the children did not, and they happily ascended the cable car content in the belief that NASA was protecting them. I did tell them the truth at the top to be greeted by the fairly common, "Oh Sir!"

Once on the main level it's a perfectly good visit if you take in the church, with the choir if you're lucky, the statue, the views and the shops, but to really get the most out of your day you need to access the higher peaks via one of the funicular railways. Our choice is always the funicular St Joan because it takes you up to the front of the mountain with the best views.

The first problem with it is the fact that, from where you are, it actually does look as if it is vertical and so some of the children simply can't be persuaded to get on it. In actual fact it is quite a gentle rise helped by the angled floors of the carriages, which allow you to stand quite comfortably.

The second problem, which isn't really, is that the staff here seem to be very Catalan indeed. The elderly gentleman who has been seeing us on to the train for many years, has never said anything that I have even begun to understand. We communicate through mime and smiling, which seems to work in most places when all else has failed.

It is a great ride, giving fabulous views of the monastery as you are literally dragged up the mountain by the hefty chains and the weight of the descending train, which you pass smoothly at the half way point.

Once up it's important to gather everyone together and give them a sense of where they are. It would be hard to fall off but…. That done, you lead the group up to the summit on the left and then over the top and down the well-made path to the series of viewing points until you are back on, what feels like, the security of the base level. An undulating, forty-five minute trek that provides the most spectacular views across the rugged landscape of Catalonia.

Montserrat takes around two to three hours to visit, and so in the afternoon we were prone to drop in to Sitges. This is a lovely seaside resort very popular with the Barcelona rich. Its old town nestles around a picturesque bay which used to provide excellent safe swimming, and the newer end has lovely beaches and, most importantly, ice cream….it was here one year that we came across an amazing collection of sand sculptures in the middle of the large beach which prompted from one young man the comment and question. "Wow, these are amazing…. where do you think they got all the sand from….?"

Barcelona

The visit here is the centre piece of all of our tours and we tend to spend two full days exploring its many sites and experiences. For the children, particularly the boys, the big event is the visit to the Nou Camp stadium, home of Barcelona FC. Even I enjoy my biannual visit even though football mostly leaves me cold. This is not just because of the immense size of the stadium, which holds 98,000 fans, but also because Barcelona really is "Mes que un club" more than just a club. The passion with which it is supported is intriguing and I really like their scheme to bring on young local players and not just buy in the world's best.

All visits there are good but one year was particularly special. On that occasion we had two coaches and the other, with my friend and colleague Roger in charge, simply couldn't find the stadium. Roger had the smart idea of hailing a cab and paying it to lead them. This worked and they soon pulled up outside. Another coach pulled in behind them and also began to off load its passengers. Ours was full of football crazy boys from Sussex, theirs contained the entire Barcelona Squad including Ronaldhino. A frenzy of autograph gathering ensued and the squad were all very happy to oblige.

Having ticked off the Nou camp, we load the children into the coach and head up Montjuic to visit the Olympic Stadium and to take in the breath taking views across the city, the visual centre of which is the Sagrada Familia.

This remarkable and very odd church has been under construction for over a hundred years since Gaudi, whose buildings all over the city give it a unique feel, designed it. We used to visit there also and take the braver members of the group up the alarming spiral staircases to get a closer look at the modernistic carvings and statues, but in recent years the building work has accelerated, as has its popularity, and currently it's too much money for too crowded and limited a space, with much of it closed off or shrouded in scaffolding.

We always, though, visit Las Ramblas, the beautiful open boulevard that stretches away from the harbour to the Plaza de Catalunya, tree-lined and spacious with a wonderful cosmopolitan feel about it. For years this was a favourite stop for lunch and shopping, particularly in the Boqueria covered market half way up that boasts the best sweet stall on earth {in the kids' opinion} and also, further in, an amazing fish market with huge octopi and lots of things I simple don't recognise but wouldn't like to meet in their natural environment.

You had to warn the children not to fall for the three cups or the three-card trick and to be careful of their bags and pockets, but they actually think that that's all part of the fun!

Buskers are also a big part of the magic of Las Ramblas, but sadly less so in recent years as those who can actually do something are replaced by living statues that just stand still! Maybe that's a possible retirement job.

The day ends with a stroll through the Gothic quarter and the inevitable wait as the coach negotiates the road system to pick us up. We've learnt over the years to allow plenty of time built in to the day to deal with that.

Chapter 6 - Alaska

Alaska, a temptingly distant fluke

An English teenager's adventures in Alaska.

Christopher South was my most regular co-traveller during his teenage years. His parents were absolutely convinced of the educational value of travel and Chris went on every trip there was, I think.

But the biggest adventure of all was our expedition to Alaska. I'd been there before, on a teacher exchange, and had a fantastic time staying with a gracious and welcoming couple called Andy and Nanci. It was all good but the best bit began with a flight up to Gastineau from Juneau in a 737 at altitudes that kept us lower than the peaks swinging up the valleys and swooping over the bays, to meet Andy in Glacier Bay aboard his yacht "Adventuress". What a beautiful boat, gleaming in the Alaskan sunlight, which is all about reflections, six berths and a wood burning stove.

We cruised back down to Juneau through the inside passage, mostly with me prone on the bowsprit watching the dolphins leaping along beneath me, and then we found some whales.

I'd never seen a whale live before, nor met anyone who had, but here I was in whale central and they were happy to play.

The first one we saw was a mother humpback, 40' of love with a tiny, sort of, calf by her side. Andy expertly drifted the yacht alongside and we sat and listened to their breathing as they rested in the shallow water.

Then the daddy whale appeared off to our left {port, sorry.} He was heading in to say "hi" to his good lady and we were in the way.

Andy yelled, "Hold on, it's gonna hit".

I grabbed the spar behind me, my gaze fixed on the grey back of the whale as it surged towards us.

Within 10 feet it dived a short way and rolled to its right bringing its eye towards the sky and me and I had my first spiritual moment with these great mammals as our gazes locked before it surged under the boat. The tail rose once and filled my vision before sliding silently beneath us and then was gone.

I was hooked and after a great month I knew that I would have to come back and with children. This was just too good to miss.

It took two years to arrange, with the help of friends we had made and Amanda Grange, who worked at County Hall, but eventually everything was in place and we were off. The final party consisted of thirty or so people from three different schools, some families, some friends, and Chris as the sole student representative of our Community College.

Closing in! Alaska

Four of us decided to break our journey in San Francisco: myself and Chris and two adult friends of mine who had been charmed by my tales of whales, bears and eagles.

What a great city! Last time we found our way to Sausalito, just across the bay, and had lunch in this seafood restaurant called Horizons, which stuck out over the water and had the best view of downtown San Francisco, so back we went.

This must be one of the best ferry crossings in the world, certainly no need to hire an expensive launch or to book a tour. With views of the Golden Gate to your left and a brief stop at two or three of the islands, including "The Rock" itself, the legendary prison of Alacatraz, sometime home to Al Capone and Robert Franklin Stroud, the Birdman.

The crossing achieved in brilliant sunshine, we landed at the dock that proudly declaims that we were in a Nuclear Free Zone. Once again we had a fabulous day in this fabulous place. Great lunch, great view, great houses, great shopping, and, of course, great company.

Then we walked back over the Golden Gate amusing ourselves in the high winds with the video camera and US road signs that appeared to be aimed at us like "No turning".

Back on terra firma, if you can call it that on the San Andreas Fault, we headed for Haight Ashbury, home of the hippies, and found some. Our closest encounter was with a man who looked as if he'd been there since forever. He was standing on the edge of the pavement and as Chris walked by came out with this classic statement,

"It's really come to something if all I get to do all day is talk to a dumb idiot like you".

Chris was naturally quite shocked as we bustled him past, until he glanced back and realised that we'd walked through an on-going dialogue that the man was having.... with his own reflection. I suspect that he's still there.

North to Alaska

So then we flew North to Alaska, all of us silenced by the endless wilderness of British Columbia and the thought of how small a piece of wilderness that actually was. It was on this flight that I first heard a member of the cabin crew come out with;

"If the cabin depressurises, masks will descend from the bulkhead above you. If you are travelling with a child affix your mask first.

If you are travelling with two children put the mask on the one you like most first."

I've heard it said since but really hope we were there for the original. He wasn't able to tell us what to do with twelve children… the others having joined us in Seattle.

We landed in Juneau in the rain. It's a strange airport with a huge runway for jets and a long canal for landing water planes, of which there were hundreds. This time I was staying with David and Maureen; which was excellent news for me. Not only were they very nice people who lived in a fabulous wooden house with a view of the passage that the liners used to enter the harbour, BUT they also owned a big boat!

We spent a few days acclimatising and resting after our flight, but it wasn't wasted time. Juneau is a fascinating place. No roads in or out, as the owner of a Winnebago which landed there found out, much to the amusement of the local people, and the State Capital. Because it is so small this means that bumping in to the Governor or having dinner at the next table to the Attorney General was a common experience. We even toured the Governor's house where Chris hung back so that he could sit on the Governors loo, but only for a photo opportunity. Mel Gibson has a house there and we are still convinced that that was Richard Chamberlain at a table across the room in an up-market harbour-side restaurant. So much so that I rang my mum, a big fan, to tell her, forgetting that we were eight or nine hours behind. At the other end of town is the Red Dog Saloon, complete with swinging doors and thousands of names scrawled on the walls, including all three members of Nirvana who, apparently, regularly visited there from their hometown of Seattle.

It just isn't possible to tell all the stories of those amazing three weeks but I will tell you six. The Channel 24 incident; the problem with bears; the boy and the whale; Skagway and the White Horse pass; encounters on Kake island; and the birth of an iceberg.

So first, Channel 24

None of us at that time were used to multi channel TV and we spent quite some time, initially, channel hoping. Whilst idly flicking through one day I came across the now legendary, at least in my circle of friends, Channel 24.

Channel 24 is dedicated to a view, the same view, day and night, winter and summer. The fixed camera stares across an expanse of water, the trees sway, birds fly past and no doubt the occasional bear or whale makes a guest appearance. Fascinating stuff, and I'm not being sarcastic, I really enjoyed watching it.

Anyway, who could resist such a temptation? David did the research and found out where the camera was and Chris and I duly booked a cab and directed him to our location. The driver was understandably curious and started ringing his family and friends and telling them to turn to Channel 24 and keep on watching.

Having arrived he sat in the cab, amused by his mad English fares, and Chris and I got into position just to the side of the camera and then, on my cue, we sidled pythonesquely in to view and began to tap dance, badly, since neither of us actually could. We did though manage some pirouettes and a few good jumps and spins before the laughter caused a general collapse, fortunately at about the same time as the man from the TV station arrived to tell us to go away, which proves somebody must watch it.

Bear Island

Then there was Admiralty Island. A huge expanse of bear-filled forest, tightly controlled by the state. Only 16 people a day are allowed to share the Island with 1000 or so Big Brown Bears. This promised great things.

Because of the licensing we had to split the party but a colleague, Chris and I ended up together. We took off in a seaplane from Juneau with two Germans sharing our flight. They unfortunately had not got a licence and were sent straight back.

The landing was interesting with spray flying by as we bounced to a sort of a halt. Then we had to wade ashore so, rather than get soaked, we tied plastic bags around our boots.

On the beach the lady ranger greeted us and we were all pleased to note the size of her gun. First off we put our lunch in bags that were then hauled high up into a tree to protect them and make us less appetising.

Then she told us to walk around the corner to a river estuary where, she said, we would find bears. She gave us advice about staying on the high ground where the bears were used to seeing people and then launched into a health and safety briefing like no other. It entertained me so much that it became a standard assembly for years afterwards. The theme being, "What to do if you are approached by a bear." Useful stuff in the South East of England. Well you never know, global warming or a need to control some other wild escapee might lead to the reintroduction of bears to the Ashdown Forest.

It went something like this, and was delivered with great panache and complete seriousness; "If you encounter a bear do not try and give it a long hard stare because the long hard stare of a large brown bear is a long hard stare too far and you will just make it cross. Lower your eyes to the ground and back off slowly. If the bear advances towards you try to keep as much space as you can between the bear and you. This may mean that you have to run but please be aware that the Grizzly bear, over rough terrain on the flat, will surely outrun you. So, if you have to run, head for the nearest sizable tree BUT do not climb that tree because bears can climb trees too and probably faster than you. Keep the tree between you and the bear because bears cannot corner worth a damn and eventually, unless you trip or tire, the bear will lose interest and wander off in search of salmon or berries.

If there is no tree and you have to run then run down hill because a bears front legs are shorter than its rear legs and, if you're lucky, the bear will stumble and give you time to get away.

If you cannot get away fall to the ground and pretend to be dead because bears don't eat carrion, if the bear takes a bite {seriously} do not react. The bear will then assume that you are dead and leave you alone……

Having listened carefully to the advice, in true English fashion we put our faith in the uniform and off we trotted, without the lady with the big gun who had to stay with the unlicensed Germans, and low and behold, just round the corner in a wide wild estuary, there were bears, lots of them. Chris and I stayed well up on the high ground whilst my colleague went a little closer, showing due scientific disregard for danger.

The bears were either sitting in the rivers and streams scooping out the fish, taking one mouthful and throwing the rest on to the bank, or, in the case of the young ones, play fighting their way… our way. The Salmon were clearly running and even though we couldn't get close on this occasion, elsewhere we had been able to witness this remarkable sight close up.

It actually is impossible to exaggerate the density of fish in these streams when the salmon are running. The rivers are literally seething, carpeted by the writhing mass that is already starting to rot. We discussed whether this early process of decay was a defense mechanism designed to protect them from the bears and the eagles long enough for them to make it to their spawning grounds. If it was it wasn't working…..

As my travelling companion strayed further and further down the slope I became a little anxious, and encouraged him to rejoin us by pointing out that if the bears came any closer I would turn and run. To which he replied that we'd been told not to do that because the bears were faster than us and the tree line looked alarmingly distant. To which I replied that I didn't care about any of that because we were faster than him.

I may not have been the first person to say this … but I said it then.

Fortunately our ranger appeared at this point with her reassuring gun and all was well. Our errant friend was called back to safety and we were allowed to pose with the gun, unloaded, with the bears splashing around in the background.

After lunch we decided to walk into the woods along a gravel path to a look out tower by a feeding stream where we could get a very close look at these huge and beautifully dangerous creatures.

As we were walking through the trees, as quietly as we could so that we didn't frighten away the bears, it suddenly occurred to us that frightening away the bears was exactly what we should be doing until we were safely up that tower with its narrow bear-proof ladder and so all of a sudden we were stomping away through the gravel and singing and whistling in a way that would have frightened away almost anything.

In due course we reached the tower and climbed to safety. Now we were quiet and anyone who spoke was duly shushed. After more than an hour our patience was rewarded when a colossus of a bear hove in to view. I say hove because that was how the bear moved, like an elegant vessel making its way up the river. Until you see one of these animals close up it's really hard to appreciate the sense of danger that they emanate. There is nothing cuddly at all about a thousand pounds of sinuous muscle, fronted by jaws that could take your leg clean off.

Our bear came very close, passing just beneath us, and we were very, very still. He, or she, looked at us in a half interested sort of way and then moved on about his, or her, business and we sighed with relief and ran back to the beach to watch our plane cruising in to the bay, sending up curtains of spray and ending up much closer to the beach than he'd managed before. Funny that.

Which takes us to the whale tail, and that isn't a spelling mistake.

The sight that tempted us in to the rowing boat. Alaska

A whale of a tale

Over dinner one evening, quite late in the trip, I was once again banging on about whales and whale watching and my experiences with Andy and Nanci the last time round and finally it worked and the offer was made.

Next morning we would all go down to the harbour and take the boat out for a spot of whale watching, hooray!

We started early and drove down to the bay. There were many boats of various types and sizes and we didn't know which one was ours for the duration as we followed hopefully along the quay. When David climbed on to a really big cabin cruiser I decided that this was already a most excellent day.

We all boarded with our excessive provisions, took off the covers and watched David expertly manoeuvre the boat into open water. Then it was our turn and we spent a happy three hours taking it in turns to Captain the ship.

It was on this day that I realised why everything in Alaska looked so big. I've been around higher mountains in many places but never mountains that rose straight from the sea. In Juneau fifteen thousand feet means exactly that, not a four thousand foot peak rising from an eleven thousand foot plateau.

Our outward journey done we turned off the engines and waited, keeping really quiet. It felt a bit like being in a waiting room and a bit like being in a great church. There was a tremendous sense of expectation.

Then Wow! Off to our left a humpback whale breached the surface and crashed to its side. There and gone before the cameras could be poised and, anyway, a little too far off to really satisfy our needs.

That though was only the start of it. Within half an hour there were twelve of these great beauties swimming in a loose lazy circle around the boat, about 50 yards away.

They flicked their flukes, they rolled onto their backs and waved their huge flippers at us, they noisily spouted their greetings in the still bright sunshine.

We were in a frenzy. I was jumping up and down and squeaking like a nine year old at the circus. I had to have more.

David said that the engines would frighten them away. "OK," said I, "What about the rowing boat?"

David agreed, so long as I wore a life jacket, after all, what's the worst that could happen?

Chris wanted to come too so we rang his mum in England and

explained our plan, which was to row into the middle of the pod and see what happened next. Great plan.

His mum was all for Chris experiencing life to the full and so she gave her permission and off we went.

Whales swim like dolphins, but on a huge and majestic scale and the key to success was going to be rowing to the place where we thought they would next appear. I was rowing away with my back to the bow and Chris was keeping lookout. The boat was about six feet long.

Trying to get out of the way. Alaska

The others were watching with interest, cameras poised.

After what seemed only a moment Chris spoke.

"I think you'd better stop." He said.

"Don't be such a wimp." I said.

"No, really, I think you should stop." His tone had changed but I was still intent on getting just a little bit closer.

Chris was a very polite boy so I was very surprised at his next statement.

"Stop rowing this ******* boat now."

That, reinforced by the white knuckled grip that he had on the edge of his seat, brought me to my senses and I turned to look.

Only a few metres away the pod was coming up and we were directly in their path. I took one huge pull with my left oar and one more with both as a leviathan of the deep broke surface where our boat had momentarily been. The blowhole, big enough to jump in, opened as it passed and blew a great gust of fishy mist in to the sky. It settled on our faces and we both laughed at being breathed on by a whale.

The back came next, a wall of glistening, streaming black blocking out the world. Down it went rolling past until the last, the tail, rose into view and actually cast its shadow on us as it sailed above us and slid without a ripple in to the calm dark sea.

We could have touched it … if we'd been able to move.

It was only moments later that we were back on board the cruiser with a glass of wine in my trembling grip. "Close enough?" David queried in his dry Alaskan way.

Oh yes, quite close enough. At least for that day.

The White Horse Pass to the Yukon

Our itinerary now placed the whole group on the coastal ferry to Skagway, famed gateway of the 1898 gold rush to the Yukon. Then tens of thousands of hopeful prospectors braved the brutal conditions of the White Horse Pass carrying their provisions on their backs if they were unlucky and using mules if they were not.

Skagway looked like a gold town should. The sidewalks were wide and wooden and the bars and restaurants could have been lifted straight out of the Wild West. We all wandered about in the two hours before our train was due, looking for lunch, of course, and found a local restaurant in a back street that served steak on gravy soaked bread, which they described as toast. Tasty and very filling.

We passed some of the time by panning for gold in a small creek, but to no avail. I suppose 150 years of prospectors had beaten us to it.

We arrived in good time to find an actual steam train with traditional carriages waiting for us and boarded eagerly. The train moved off smoothly and we were soon beginning the climb of three thousand feet in twenty or so miles.

This must be one of the world's most spectacular railroads, twisting as it does through the rugged landscape across gorges on trestles and through tunnels that take you by surprise. The views drop away alarmingly as you get higher and the steam makes it all feel very real. Finally the Yukon hoves in to view and turns out to be a boggy terrain, wreathed in mist. Damp, cold and uninviting to us in our thermals and boots after our hot lunch and comfortable journey, how daunting must it have seemed to the original prospectors who had hoofed it up the pass? They though, we supposed, were fired up with gold fever and probably didn't mind.

Kake Island

A few days passed and it was time to pay a visit to Kake Island, where one of our initial hosts had been the Principal. This was well off the beaten track and promised a taste of the reality of living in an isolated community.

On the way down we all fell foul of an odd Alaskan law. One of the kids called out, "Look, there's a Moose!" and indeed there

Sawyer Glacier Calving. We estimated the Glacier to be about 400 feet

was. It was a small plane and the pilot overheard. I think he waited for such opportunities as he managed to deliver his warning with a straight face that looking at a moose out of the window of an aircraft was an offence in that state, as was pushing a moose from a moving plane.....

The approach was interesting. As our small plane began its decent we noticed a black spot on the runway. This turned out to be a large black bear, who was enjoying the heat rising off the tarmac. Our pilot didn't seem at all phased and just bussed across it a couple of times, executing some acrobatic turns in the process, until it got the message and made its unhurried progress in to the bushes.

Having landed we walked up the road to the village school where we were introduced to a group of local teenagers, all Native

The Birth of an Iceberg in Tracey Arm. Alaska

Americans. We all sat and chatted and we quickly sensed their frustrations with life on the island where they spent their evenings riding up and down the only road in their trucks and talking to each other, pointing out that it was impossible to have a serious relationship when everyone was everyone else's cousin. They were fascinated by tales of cinemas and burger bars and seemed despondent that their only chance of employment was in the salmon processing plant that we were to visit later in the day.

We all went for a walk together and one of them asked us if we would like to meet the Chief of their Tribe. We all enthusiastically said that we would and so we were taken in to a large workshop where a very large man was carving a totem pole with a hand held chisel. He looked every inch the Chief and was most gracious; giving us slivers of the sacred wood to take home with us. Mine is still on the shelf in my office. One of the students asked him if he could tell us his name. We expected something along the lines of "Black Eagle' or "He Who Wrestles Bears". He was actually called

Michael Jackson.

The Birth of an Iceberg

Tracey Arm Fjord was to be the site of our last adventure. A commercial boat trip this time, which took us south from Juneau and up the inlet until we were floating beneath the immense mass of the twin Sawyer Glaciers.

They seemed to me to be hundreds of feet high and we were at a safe distance, waiting for the calving process to provide a spectacular display. We were not to be disappointed. Patience is the key in these situations and we stood and waited and watched. The glaciers actually breathe and the wheezing and hissing of the moving ice fills the air. Small pieces came free and fell as the inexorable process continued and then a huge segment broke free and ponderously and thunderously crashed into the sea, sending small boats that had been a little too brave bouncing and pitching as the pressure wave pushed them aside. The great mountain of ice disappeared beneath the waves and then breached the surface like a playful humpbacked whale.

We had witnessed the birth of an iceberg, which would now make its way slowly down the fjord to begin its long journey somewhere.

On the way out we passed a line of smaller icebergs, each one a brilliant blue in the Alaskan sunshine and some playing host to seals and sea birds as they went.

Seattle

With all farewells complete and genuine promises to return, or host a visit to England made, we set off on our return journey. This time we were to break our journey properly in Seattle, the city of Microsoft and Boeing.

We were only there for one brief day so we had to be selective in what we did and decided to visit the Old Seattle Underground, yet another unique experience for all of us.

In 1889 a fire destroyed much of down town Seattle. In planning the rebuild, the City Fathers decided to kill two birds with one stone, the other being regular flooding, by re-building in brick and stone and raising the street level by a whole storey.

Concrete piles were duly constructed and the new street level laid upon them. This left a large area of old Seattle entombed and abandoned, effectively sealing off the ground floor of many surviving buildings and creating a time capsule for future explorers to enjoy. Wandering through the dusty rooms is an eerie experience made even stranger by the sympathetic oil lighting. Odd to think that those seats were probably last sat on by some adventurer heading north into the wilderness one hundred years before.

Chapter 7 - Florida

Once you've been to Disney in Paris any number of times, what do you do next? The answer is to give in to the polite "demands" of our travelling children and set up a visit to Florida, so we did. Sadly there is no cheap way of doing this and even with car washing schemes and other support around the college only seven students were able to come.

A long flight to Miami and a tedious transfer later we were checked in to our rooms on International Drive and, armed with our theme park vouchers and free minibuses, we were set to go.

We all agreed that Disney itself was a bit tired, but the other parks were spectacular. Seaworld gave us our first {and to date only} encounter with Killer Whales, but we would rather have seen them in the wild.

The only other thing of note was the amazing holographic laser displays that ended the day at that park and, of course, breakfast at Denny's.

We had been told we couldn't miss this and so we didn't and all eight of us soon got used to ordering our eggs over and easy and our pancakes with ice cream and syrup. We certainly were ready before we left to "have a nice day now".

The real highlight of the week though was a nighttime trip to watch the launch of the Space Shuttle, Discovery, which was to be sent off on its three million mile journey to rendezvous with the Russian space station, Mir.

You can know the meaning of words and phrases without actually really understanding them. Understanding comes through experience. On this night we were to discover the meaning of "awe" and "take your breath away".

Days earlier we were intrigued to learn that the Discovery was to be launched in the early hours, in fact shortly after midnight, which promised an even more intense experience. We decided that this was a must-do and so, with the help of our helpful tour guide, we arranged a minibus to drive us through the night from Orlando to the nearest viewing point that we could reach.

The two and half hour journey timed to get us there just before midnight on February 2nd, was in itself fascinating, as we left the glare of the themed streets of Orlando and headed out in to the alligator filled darkness. It wasn't quite "Deliverance", well to be fair it wasn't "Deliverance" at all, but it felt like it to us.

The minibus was warm and soporific and it wasn't long before the young travellers drifted off to sleep leaving the driver and me chatting in to the night, equally interested in each other's lives and culture. The roads were flat and straight and the headlights did pick up the reflective eyes of the alligators in the ditches either side. One of the kids did stir and ask if we could stop so they could relieve themselves in the darkness, I said "no" but did explain why which distracted them all because now, very much awake, they spent the rest of the journey looking for more of these scaly monsters, ironic given our experiences in the Amazon a few years later.

As we approached Cape Canaveral the density of cars and people began to increase. We were lucky in that the driver clearly knew his way around. Perhaps this was a local and lucrative cottage industry, a suspicion backed up by the fact that we had to pay an "entrance fee" to get in to the ordinary unmarked car park to a man, casually dressed, with no sign of badge or uniform.

Warmly dressed against the chill we disembarked and made our way to the bank of a muddy, and no doubt alligator-infested creek. The raised position gave us a clear view across the flat marshy landscape towards the launch site.

Other launch watchers, clearly more experienced, were happy to turn up the volume on their transistor radios and hand us cups of steaming strong coffee from their many thermoses. If the numbers on our stretch of road were repeated all around that massive perimeter there must have been tens of thousands of spectators for this remarkable event.

The night was moonless and extra dark with pretty much continuous cloud cover, but at a good height.

Ways away, so far it was the size of a small dinky toy, The Discovery and the launch tower that supported and nourished it, shone in the bright arc lights that surrounded them.

Steam and smoke were escaping from the tower and shuttle and the commentary from the control room made the whole thing feel surreal and filmic. We stood silently waiting as the countdown entered the last minute. As it passed ten seconds everyone, ourselves included, began to join in and then, on one, the engines fired. We all took an involuntary step backwards, startled by the white-hot intensity of the burn. It is no exaggeration to say that, for a few magical moments, night turned in to day. The clouds were lit as if by sunlight and you could easily have read a book several miles distant. It was made even more eerie by the complete silence. No noise from the crowd after the universal sharp intake of breathe, and no noise from the rocket either. As the monumental clouds of smoke and steam erupted in all directions the sound arrived, a physical force that blew through our hair and felt like a hot summer's wind in our faces. Nobody moved until, after what seemed like an hour, but was probably only a moment, the tower disengaged and fell away and the Discovery began to rise unfeasibly slowly from the ground. At that moment the cheering began and rose as the spaceship rose on its own self-lit path. As it picked up speed it seemed to be almost falling and we were all anxious until we realised that it was just heading for the horizon at an astonishing speed, and then it shot in to the clouds, which were lit for a moment as it passed, and then it was gone. Probably no more than two minutes of our lives from 12.22.04 on February 3rd 1995. Absolutely awesome and our breath was briefly, physically, taken away.

All the way back to Orlando and pretty much ever since we have been trying to work out how to describe it to people who weren't there so that they get a sense of what it was like. I hope finally, almost twenty years later, I've come close.

Chapter 8 - Borneo

A big part of our experience in Borneo was the week we spent living with the locals in a jungle village of traditional raised long houses in the Kelabit highlands of Malaysia close to the border of Indonesia.

Getting there was itself a challenge. First the endurance feat of the seemingly endless flight from London, admittedly made easier by the luxurious Jumbo we were carried by to Kuala Lumpur, where sadly we never left the airport, and then the shorter and much more spectacular flights, first across the South China Sea to Kuching and then over the coastal rainforests to Sibu and then finally to Miri where we experienced our first "trek," 10 minutes across Miri to the bus station. This involved crossing a number of large roads. Strangely though, even though the traffic was quite busy, this was easy and quite stress free. The drivers treated pedestrians like other cars and gave way politely as you crossed. No blaring horns and revving engines here.

Borneo, a river view.

The team had already shopped, girls on groceries and boys on knives and hardware {their choice} so we were ready to go. The bus was air-conditioned and the seats well padded so we settled down for our forty five minute ride into the jungle.

As we climbed, the houses became fewer and the trees more exotic until we arrived at the Lambir Hills, a National Park some way down the coast.

The coach left us at the gate and we trekked up the shallow gradient. This took five minutes and then we waited, trying to catch our breath, whilst the daily leader checked us in. Then we trekked for 2 minutes more to our exclusive chalet with its two bedrooms, a lounge area and a loo. I don't think we really appreciated how much of a luxury that was.

View of the toilet, Village in Borneo

That night we had our first meal of noodles and garlic, made more palatable by the selection of fresh vegetables the girls had bought in the market. Noodles were to be a recurring theme of our journey and it was here that I coined the phrase "Think Fuel Not Food" which was to return to haunt me many times. Having said it I had to eat the slimy little pieces of tasteless plastic soaked in a powdery soup without comment or complaint, on numerous occasions, and I did, mostly.

This was cooked on an open fire in the large wok that we took turns to carry.

Borneo – A picture of a strange plant.

Our guide had given us excellent advice about mosquitoes along the lines that sprays don't work because you sweat them off almost instantly, but reeking of garlic did, and he was right. You could actually see them pulling out of their biting runs as soon as they hit the enveloping stench that we were soon all enclosed by.

For the next few days we explored the walks in the surrounding hills. It certainly was a beautiful place but strangely quiet, except at dawn and dusk when the invisible insects and alleged monkeys created a positive cacophony. I, for one, was glad that I had put in all those hours in the gym. Ten years older than anyone else in the group I was very conscious of the need to keep up.

The most impressive of acclimatisation treks took us in to the Niah Caves National Park, the entrance to which was a short bus journey away, three kilometres north of the town of Batu Niah. Not ones for making life easy for ourselves we walked the long way around a massive outcrop that did provoke a conversation about "The Lost World' of Arthur Conan-Doyle and the possibility of dinosaurs, we could but hope for at least a large lizard of some variety, or a bird, or anything. We did though have some wild life encounters that built to a spectacular finale.

We had been warned about a particularly venomous but very small snake, which the locals referred to as a "bootlace snake," so we were very much on our guard, although now years after I doubt their word, a bit of teasing I think. Anyway, we moved stealthily down the well-worn track through the ancient forest, so well worn that the young explorers were leading the way and we were taking up the rear. After we had all passed a particular spot, our guide, loudly, called us back. Lying on the track in several well trodden pieces was indeed a small black snake that did look a bit like a bootlace, or maybe an over extended tadpole. It was very dead. To this day we don't know whether we actually killed it by our careless stomping or whether it was just lying there as we passed over it. Later we found a small green snake, dead, and some time later, as we walked down the long raised wooden pathway through the forest towards the entrance to the caves, we think we saw a sloth hanging from a branch in the middle distance, which may as well have been dead for all it did. We watched it for half an hour and detected no movement at all!

Borneo Opening of the Niah Cave just before sunset

Nevertheless we had high hopes of the later part of our day. The Niah caves are a huge complex with large amounts of interesting evidence of prehistoric habitation dating back forty thousand years, but we were there primarily because of the birds and the bats.

As we explored the suitably cavernous interior of these limestone caverns we were struck by the lack of Stalagmites or Stalactites {g for ground and c for ceiling, in case you were wondering} but were very impressed by the immense amount of guano through which we were wading, perhaps the stories were true.

Borneo - View of the surprising rice paddies at Bario

As dusk approached we joined the small group of travellers who had gathered by the entrance, staying just inside so that the darkening sky was framed by the limestone and anything that flew in or out would briefly be in silhouette. Our patience was finally to be rewarded. First there were a few, then a few thousand and then who knows how many, two hundred and fifty thousand or so I'm told, a constant stream of small swiftlets seeking a safe roost for the night. Disappearing in to the welcoming, to them, interior.

Moments later the main event began. From deep within came the whirring flutter of bat wings, faintly threatening for westerners brought up on a diet of vampire movies, and the bats began their zigzagging scatter into the night to forage in the local forests. It was an astonishing sight and sound. An actual cloud of bats stretching off into the night and lasting for minutes. At home one bat in the garden caused excitement and now we were witnessing one of the wonders of the natural world, something which has been happening at dawn and dusk for fifty thousand years. Impossible to film or photograph, you simply have to be there. Amazing.

A few days later and a few pounds lighter, we had successfully acclimatised, a real physical process which goes far beyond just "getting used to it" and we were ready for the real trekking and project phases of the expedition so it was back to the airport for another flight, this time in a tiny propeller-driven plane which held about fourteen people. We were soon in the air flying over rainforest broken only by rivers and occasional areas of logging.

We had a discussion about that during which one of the students asked a very relevant question, which was, "how much of Europe used to be covered in forest before the Europeans cut it all down?"

Eventually we made our approach and landed successfully at Bario airport. A place that felt incredibly remote. One grass airstrip and a control tower that was part shed and part tent occupied by a group of very young and smiley soldiers.

Our packs were thrown in the back of a truck and we began the walk in to Bario Village. Bario was then a one-horse town: one main

Borneo Rope Bridge to the village
{referred to as worthy of Jurassic park}

street, one spur road, one shop and one hostel, which was to be our accommodation for the night. One room, no beds, but a view over the paddy fields that we were all surprised to find at over six thousand feet.

Once we had retrieved our packs but not unpacked {the longer you leave your sleeping bag unrolled the more likely you are to find that you are sharing it} we went down to the communal area, which consisted of a few simple tables and chairs, or so we thought.

After a short walk around the village we were returning to the hostel, hoping for some hot food and a coolish drink, when the surprising hum of a generator began to emanate from behind the building. As we walked in some of the friendly guys were pulling back a pair of wooden shutters

The Rope Bridge. Borneo

half way up one of the walls, to reveal, to my amazement and some sense of disappointment, the largest flat screen TV I had ever seen. Cold drinks were handed out from the fridge out the back and everyone settled down to noisily watch the match, which I think was England v Holland, but I wouldn't swear to it. It would seem we would have to go further to find our primitive culture but for that night, that was just fine.

The following morning, after a night on the boards under nets, we donned our packs and set off down the dusty road into the jungle. Conversation fell away as the heat of the day mounted and we all focused on the job in hand, which was just getting there, wherever there was. To this day I don't know the name of the village we stayed in or the old man whose family house became our home. We all though do recall their courteous and kind ways.

The village was approached by a rope bridge worthy of Jurassic Park and consisted of several long lodges, raised on poles, around a large central clearing where water buffalo roamed unfettered.

Borneo. The buildings are the village where we built the path for the portly Priest. The end window of the large building was the room 15 of us slept in.

Closing off the circle was a small wooden hotel where we were to be offered tea and cake on more than one occasion.

Our accommodation was one room, with one double bed and one unglazed window, so we made ourselves comfortable and then went through to dinner, an extensive meal which included every conceivable part of a chicken and the greens off the tops of the vegetables, possibly potatoes, that we generally consider inedible and throw away but which were actually very palatable. The chicken coup was just outside the door next to the ramshackle toilet and it got emptier by the day. I think the young travellers made the connection but I'm not entirely sure…

Next day we were to begin our project, which could have been any one of a number of environmentally helpful tasks, and in some ways I suppose it was.

At one end of the village were two larger buildings. One, built on the ground, was a small church, and the other, some thirty feet or so away, was the house of the Priest. It is worth noting that Christianity came here late and we had already had one old man pointed out to us as a reformed cannibal and head hunter, although I'm not sure that any of us believed it.

The problem was that the ground between the house and the church was very wet and so our project was to build a raised path of turf and earth from one building to the other, and since the gentleman in question was quite portly, it would have to be well made and quite wide.

The villagers all turned out. The adult men to stand, watch, smoke and commentate, and everybody else to pitch in and help, and this is where it got interesting.

Water buffalo roam the village

They divided themselves into teams of the right number. One group of teenage boys used mattocks to cut out turfs and break up soil from a rough area to one side. A second team, mostly of young girls, worked in pairs with each holding two corners of a sack so that it could be used to carry soil, much more efficient than filling and emptying them. A third team formed a line and passed turfs down it from the cutting area to the fourth and final team who then edged the new path with the turfs and packed it with the soil.

We were already impressed by the natural organisation and divided ourselves out amongst the various groups.

As time went on it became clear that something unusual and fundamentally different was happening. As soon as any one of the villagers had a moment to spare, perhaps whilst their sack was loaded or because they were waiting for turf, they moved smoothly and without comment into another team where they could be of use, the default job being to stamp down the soil already laid.

Apart from the moments we were responsible for, until we caught on, not a minute was wasted all morning.

At ten we stopped for tea and snacks, at twelve for a substantial lunch, and then we all went swimming, after which the young adventurers played Volleyball with the local lads, using the net and balls that we had brought with us as a gift to the village, interrupted only by the strolling buffalo passing through.

My view of teamwork changed that first day, as did the view of us all, and we are all the better for it.

Trekking

We had planned to use the village as the base for our main trek through the surrounding jungle and so, in due course, with full packs and boots tightly laced against the promised leeches, we set off.

The problem with rain forests is not the rain itself, funnily enough, which comes at a predictable time in the afternoon and is warm and refreshing. The rain though does cause streams that cut little valleys and I don't think we walked on flat ground at all for days. Climbing the little slopes was a problem. The natural thing to do is to grab a small tree or bush and pull yourself up and that's what we did, until our guide gently pointed out that shaking the trees was a good way to guarantee something living and probably venomous landing on your head. We made ourselves walking poles instead and made

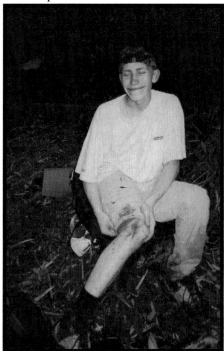

Borneo. Sam's first leech bite

what we regarded as reasonable progress. On reflection we were so slow that the guides had time to pop home for some tea and catch us at the next valley mouth.

We had encountered leeches earlier but now we seemed to be in the leech capital of the world. My record was seventeen on one leg and twenty-three on the other and other members of the party weren't far behind! Add to that one on my neck wiggling up towards my cheek and you begin to understand the horror! Nothing keeps them out or away. If you sat on your pack to rest they began to foot their way toward you, moving by reaching forward, gripping the earth and then pulling the back half up. They could get through the tightest of gaffer-taped boots and lay in wait on branches and leaves. Ordinary leeches were bad enough but the tiger leeches, with their distinctive stripe, were truly foul and actually evolutionarily challenged. Normal leeches bite and feed and fall off unnoticed, having anaesthetised the wound. Tiger leeches actually hurt and so were much more regularly removed with a quick squirt of Deet and stomped on. This was the only use we found for mosquito repellent. I got used to letting the black ones feed and fall off after a while but most of the kids couldn't bare it and we had to stop every ten minutes so they could de-leech each other.

Thunderstorm beneath Mount Kinabalu

On we trekked for day after day through the empty jungles. When I asked if there was any chance of seeing a big snake the guide looked at me as if I was mad and said that they knew when the dogs had found one whilst out hunting because five dogs went out and only four came back. I asked where all the wild life was and they said they had eaten most of it, but I suspect in reality we were just too noisy.

Finally, after days of Noodles, we made camp by a vast clump of bamboo and our native guide took pity on us. He asked us if we would like some meat and even the vegetarians amongst us couldn't resist. He disappeared soundlessly in to the jungle and soon the sound of his gun being fired reverberated through the trailing vines. Moments later he reappeared and to our horror we saw that he had Bambi draped around his shoulders. The question asked by the Sex Pistols sprang to mind and now we knew the answer. "Who killed Bambi?"…We did, and then we ate him in a stew that gave all of us two good meals. I'm not proud of that day but at the time nothing had ever tasted so good.

Our trek was coming to an end and we were camped close to a town for our last night. Our guide and the local expert had gone in to check the post and we were alone. Night fell and we were rolled up in our hammocks, at which we were now expert, then something woke me up. I could hear a snuffling, grubbing sort of sound and lay there wondering what to do. Should I look and see what it was? Might it be dangerous? I didn't have a clue so I lay still and waited, having decided that I wouldn't move unless one of the young explorers reacted in distress. The animal scrabbled about for a while and then disappeared off into the night and, eventually, I slept. In the morning the tracks, so I'm told, were those of a Pangolin, a large version of an armadillo. Completely

Borneo. Sam conquers Mount Kinabalu

harmless and quite fascinating but I'm still sure that I did the right thing. Do big snakes make those sorts of noises? I wasn't about to find out.

With the panic over and our packs packed we trekked out of the jungle and in to town and found, would you believe, a KFC. All our resolves to remain ethnic went out of the window and it was chicken wings all round.

Dawn Breaks on Mt Kinabalu

The Mountain in the Mist
Mount Kinabalu dominates everything around it, other mountains, the rainforest, and the people; even the weather. It was to be our final challenge of the Borneo expedition. Thirteen thousand five hundred feet with stripped down, but still very heavy rucksacks. Up to eleven thousand on day one and the final leg in the hours before dawn on day two, so that we could watch the sunrise from the "lonely" peak, along with all the other thrill-seekers ranging from twelve year olds with their parents to an entire coach load of geriatric Japanese tourists, BUT, we would do it faster and we would do it with heavy packs on our backs, so that was OK.

We began the day with a particularly large breakfast of…..
noodles. After I had heated them up in our large wok and added
the powdered chicken "flavouring" and several cloves of garlic,
I chased off a giant rhinoceros beetle and served up my fellow
travellers' repast, then took my steaming bowl outside to "eat" whilst
looking up at the mountain's peaks, of which there are several. With
a deft, hypocritical flick of the wrist I chucked my noodles in to
a convenient bush and ate a banana instead. Lots of slow release
calories to get me through the day. It would have to do.

It was OK actually, even though the porters carrying supplies to
the eleven thousand feet up in the air Hotel were regularly passing
us going up and down and up again with very large baskets full of
beer on their backs whilst smoking, we still felt we were pushing
ourselves.

This wasn't a climb so much as a very steep walk. The first part of
day one was the four thousand roughly hewn rock steps. These had
rest areas every fifty yards or so and in that heat and humidity they
were well used, by us and by some interesting jungle ratty things
that looked like over-sized gerbils.

The "toilets" were corrugated huts for one that were so full
of poo that you
couldn't even stand
in them without an
accidental encounter
with someone else's
droppings.

Kinabalu from the Rain Forest

This, even so, really
wasn't a problem and
as the winding path
took us from ridge to
ever-higher ridge and
the mountain range
and the rainforest began to spread out beneath us our sense of awe
and wonder increased.

After a month of lugging the packs around we were very lean and
very fit and, two hundred feet at a time, we made our way slowly
towards the rest stop. A bizarre spread of buildings around a quite

nice Hotel, by which I mean it had a bar, a restaurant, glass in the windows, and a hanging balcony from which the views down the mountain in to the valley ten thousand feet below, were astonishing. That evening we all stood there, testing the theory that you would feel the effect of one can of beer at that height because the air was thinner {this is true!} whilst watching the tropical sun set through a circular thunderstorm that filled the sky beneath us. The networks of lightning bolts and the almost ceaseless crash of thunder through the whirlpool of deeply purple clouds were transiently beautiful and we all felt glad that we were above it, not below. The Gods of Olympus never had it so good.

And then came the night…

I don't think any group of tourists on a mountain has ever been so cold. We slept in small cells off an unheated corridor; the windows did have glass, but only horizontal slats with

Dawn off Mount Kinabalu

BIG gaps. Each bed had a mattress, a pillow and a blanket and we were very high up, above the clouds beneath the clear, fantastic, unrecognizable stars. This was not good.

Before I rolled into my bunk, looking like a giant green slug with a blue nose {my hat poking out the top} I had prepared myself as best I could. Light cotton socks under light thermal long socks under heavy thermal longer socks. A full set of army thermals, cotton trousers, two light tee shirts, a heavy sweat-shirt bought in Alaska, a gortex-lined fleece, a windproof outer jacket, my thermal blue hat pulled down to the neck, two pairs of thermal gloves, my light jungle sleeping bag and a heavy, larger bag supplied by the hotel. I'd even managed a meal of the dreaded sloppy noodles. You would have thought that would do but no, I spent the whole "night", which was actually about 11pm to 2am, wide awake and shivering as the chill winds that circled the mountain showed complete distain for my preparations and found any slight chink in my armour to attack me. The kids were no better off and we all gave up at about the same time and went back in to the unheated kitchen to make coffee and get ready for the day.

The first part of the final two thousand two hundred feet was a steep rocky incline that claimed our first three casualties. One of the girls wouldn't go on because, "she had a bad feeling", one of the boys couldn't go on because his feet were so painful, and so one of our staff, had to stay with them.

The rest of us went on into the dark alien night across a landscape of bare rock and black holes and precipices. We were carrying only the lightest of packs with mainly first aid and emergency equipment.

The path zigzags up the mountain, which is designed to make you think you've reached the top only to reveal another, and another, rock plateau. Some of it, even so, is so steep or narrow that there are ropes to cling on to as you edge along, trying not to focus on the lights in the valley ten thousand feet below.

We were doing well, with the aid of our anti-nausea drugs, and even though we had become strung out we were all in sight and enjoying the astonishing views as dawn began to break over the lesser peaks of the Crocker Range below us.

At one point Sam, who was then fifteen, just lay down and gave up. It took a while to get him up, which was only achieved when I pointed out that, if he stopped, I also had to at which point he smiled at me and set off like a gazelle, leaving me trudging slowly up behind.

Eventually, exhausted, elated and triumphant we joined the queue to stand on the highest point and all took photos of each other and every conceivable view, before setting off briskly down the slopes, now in full daylight.

This time we could see the drops and we were thankful that we hadn't been able to on the way up. We were so happy that we forgot to take our pills until the intense tingling in our fingers reminded us.

Back at the Hotel we dumped all of our cooking utensils and heavy kit in the pile of "gifts" to the mountain porters, happy to have used them on our treks and challenges but equally happy in the knowledge that all that was behind us, and set off down the path.

Strangely, going down was actually harder as gravity jarred our already bruised knees again and again, but we made it in good time, commiserating as we went with the line of mountaineers going the other way.

Once the base camp had been achieved we set off for the hot springs at Poring to soak away the pain. Here the naturally heated waters are channelled into concrete tubs and troughs of varying sizes, and we wallowed happily in these natural Jacuzzis for hours reminiscing about the trip and staring at the cloud wreathed mountain above us.

Kinabalu view from the top

Mixing with the Monkeys

Having conquered Mount Kinabalu we were now into the less physical phase of our expedition and we were all very excited to be visiting the Orang-utan reserve at Sepilok, on the Eastern coast of Malaysian Borneo, world famous for its work in protecting and preserving the dwindling Orang-utan population.

After our hearty breakfast of more {expletives deleted} noodles with powdered chicken broth {with most of the powder in one lump} we set off for the rangers hut where about thirty other tourists joined us. A short walk on rickety, raised platforms through the dark and empty forest later we reached the feeding platforms where, low and behold, there were Orang-utans in all their splendour. No big males but two mums and a couple of babies.

These old women of the jungle knew no fear of us and strolled happily through the crowd as the crowd backed away to allow them passage under the watchful eye of the park rangers.

For half an hour the cameras whirred and clicked away as the monkeys displayed their charms, feeding on the bunches of bananas that had been used

Close Encounter of the Hairy Kind. Sepilok

to tempt them in, and then they were gone, leaving us with a distant view of some gibbons on a feeding platform and a distinct sense of awe.

We went back to our hut sort of happy, but feeling a bit like we'd been to the zoo.

After lunch {noodles} we decided to go for a walk in the rain forest in the hope of a more natural experience of the wildlife that was clearly there to be seen, if only we could be quiet enough. Hmm.

We filled in the relevant forms and set off into the Reserve. The kids talked happily of what they might see, loudly enough to

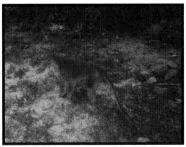

make sure that they didn't see it. Eventually we stopped and decided to sit in silence for a while to see if anything would appear. We did, it didn't, and so, an hour later, we set off for home.

The paths we followed, by pure luck, took us back to the feeding platforms where we had enjoyed our earlier, managed encounter, but this time there were no rangers

Borneo.The thieving Monkey from the beach in the South China Sea

and no tourists, except us, but there were monkeys all over the place. The Orang-utans were back and now they wanted to play, seemingly as curious about us as we were about them.

We kept a respectful distance as these beautiful cousins roamed about, sometimes on all fours and sometimes standing, and gradually we became dispersed as we followed our favoured animal. Looking back it's odd that none of us for even a moment felt any threat, even though we were in the company of large females with their babies. Something in their eyes and their gentle manner must have subconsciously calmed any fears we might have had.

Feeding platform at Sepilok

I was standing watching the gathering of Gibbons in a nearby tree when I heard a worried and worrying "Gareth, please come here".

I hurried around the corner to find Sam face to face, and I mean face to face, with a huge female Orang-utan. It was one of those moments when the world seems to recede but even so, I felt absolutely confident that everything would be fine. Sam, I think was less sure.

The rangers had given us advice before our supervised encounter, which Sam had clearly forgotten.

"Don't touch her", I said, "and back away slowly towards me".

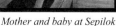
Mother and baby at Sepilok   *Strange sky line. Kelabit Highlands. Borneo.*

After what seemed like a very long time Sam took a hesitant half step back and the monkey took a confident half step forward. Another half step back, another half step forward. I almost expected music to start playing.

"Get out of her way.....Move to the side, she only wants to pass by." This was the advice we had been given. This was the Orang-utan's territory and they stood aside for no man.

Sam took an exaggerated step to his left and his new friend, complete with baby, strolled nonchalantly past, swung up on to the railings and disappeared almost instantly in to the canopy.

Our wild life quota now very much fulfilled, we retreated with dignity to the safety of our hut and the comfort of our evening meal, noodles.....

Some years later I bumped in to Sam at Eastbourne's Sovereign Harbour and, funnily enough, discussing the encounter above was very much the centre piece of our conversation.

Koto Kinabalu

Koto Kinabalu is an odd place and that's pretty much all there is to say about it. My colleague and I decided, after one night in a Hostel, to boost the reserves of the trip so that we could end our month in Borneo in style, so we booked rooms in the Hyatt Regency for all of us, keeping the price sensible by opting for multiple occupancy of the air-conditioned, en-suite rooms. We knew we were in a classy place when the reception staff didn't bat an eyelid when we walked in after a month in the jungle and looking like it. We had it confirmed when we bought a round of drinks in the piano bar later…

Our final target was a bit of rest and relaxation on one of the nearby islands so we booked a water taxi and bounced off across the South China Sea, which, I believe, has one of the highest concentrations of sharks in the world.

On arrival we waded ashore, donned our sarongs and chilled. At one point a languid Iguana strolled out of the jungle and through our party, and later a roguish Monkey robbed us, but nobody cared. We took it in turns to snorkel with our one mask and it was only when it was my turn that I realised that the protective shark net didn't in fact offer any protection at all. I should have realised that when the boat moored at the small jetty inside it. Thankfully no sharks appeared and I can only suppose that the locals know what they are doing.

Next day that was that. We set off for the airport and the long journey home, our adventure in Borneo completed.

Chapter 9 - Peru

Lima

After a night in a barracks in Hounslow and a very long flight via Lisbon and over the endless Amazon and then amazing views of the Andes we landed at Lima. I was initially disappointed by the lack of Paddington Bear memorabilia until I made the comment, only to be met by blank stares. A hair-raising taxi ride later and we were ensconced in our hostel and watching an American film dubbed in to spanish with English subtitles. We all decided that an exploratory walk was preferable and so set off. What struck us most was the fact that every house seemed to be enclosed by a wall and barbed wire, and these weren't big houses. Looking for a meal we stumbled into a friendly restaurant with a happy guitar-playing chef, who entertained us with his music and his food, which allowed us to ignore the sirens and screeching tyres, which seemed to typify an evening in the Peruvian capital. I'm sure those sounds were cars back firing.

Lima by flight

After a fascinating visit to the South American Explorers Club {I still have the jacket which doesn't fit} to check our maps and arrangements, we were good to go and that evening we caught a night bus to Huaraz which, at ten thousand and thirteen feet above sea level, was to be the centre for our acclimatisation treks. I once again proved that I can sleep between a rock and a hard place and arrived reasonably refreshed after our eight-hour journey. Having checked in, the party went to sleep, so I went out to explore. Huaraz in 2004 was a town of two halves and may well still be so. I wandered first in to the monumental town square where I found a lady with a tame Llama selling the opportunity to stroke it, which I declined.

Huaraz

Then I wandered down the street and down the hill until I crossed the rocky river and found the other side of Huaraz. The banks carried clear evidence of a lack of sewers or any means of rubbish disposal and the tiny people just looked really poor. I came across a market and wandered in. Down one side there was a long trestle table with two wooden benches. At the top was a boiling pot of something and people were having breakfast. My obvious interest resulted in friendly but incomprehensible greetings and a space was made. I sat myself down and was presented with a bowl of vegetables in a hot liquid { sorry but that's the best I can do} and a chunk of flat bread. Each time I emptied it, it was refilled, until I realized that leaving some was the queue to them to stop filling it up. Completely stuffed I took out some money to pay, notes of course, only for the very old lady to my left to pull out some change to show me how much my breakfast had cost. I had nothing like that so gave them the smallest note I had, which I think paid for the breakfast of everyone there. This point was reinforced later in the day when we were shopping for food in the market. We tried to buy potatoes with a small note only to be presented with a huge sack. By now we had some small coins and managed to buy a sensible amount. It was clear that many visitors never realised that coins that small actually existed, and that the local price structure sat almost invisibly under the apparent one. Certainly if you only ate and shopped around the main square, you would never know.

A couple of acclimatisation treks later and feeling ready to go on to our next adventure, we decided to celebrate with a meal in a restaurant as opposed to cooking something ourselves on the roof. Wandering about we found one that was offering what we thought we sought, "Piquante Coy con Patatas Fritas," a delicacy of the Peruvian Andes, spicy guinea pig and chips. Big mistake, Big.

We had seen the overcrowded cages in the markets and knew from our research that this was what the locals ate, but I don't think we really appreciated what we were doing. Nevertheless we went in and duly ordered a portion each. The restaurant was small with just a petition between the cooking area and us and soon there was the sound of "squeak, squeak, squeak, wrench and tiisssh" as our meals were dispatched and dropped in the deep fat fryer. At this point one of the boys gave up and left, followed by a member of staff to make sure he was OK, and the rest of us waited. In due course our meal appeared. Half a deep-fried guinea pig each and a pile of chips. I had a top half complete with teeth and tiny claws. I managed one shred of the dark meat and a handful of chips before I led the charge for the door. Definitely a culinary bridge too far. Weeks later, on a bus elsewhere, I was chatting to a man returning home from University who confided in me his opinion of the mountain folk who "eat jungle rats and drink pisco". To each his own.

Duly fortified we set off for our challenge of the expedition, our attempt to complete the Santa Cruz circuit.

Cordilliera Blanca. Above Huaraz

On top of the World

The Santa Cruz pass runs through the Andes in the Ancash region. Even though we were there in high summer we spent most of the trek surrounded by high snow capped peaks and the nights were very cold.

We were attempting a four-day trek through this spectacular landscape, peaking at fourteen thousand five hundred feet as we crossed Punta Union trekking from Yungay to Cashapampa.

As with all of these challenges, they were more or less challenging depending on how you did them. On this one we were part of a constant stream of tourists trekking the route, although having said that there were moments when there was nobody in sight but us.

Our fellow travellers varied from super-strong big Scandinavian blokes with full packs on their backs who leapt from rock to rock, to the old lady who bathed naked in the mountain streams and slept under a tarpaulin, through us with our donkey train to carry our main packs to the overweight camera-packing types who did the whole thing being led on horseback to the next ready-set-up camp, with dinner on the stove. There was, though, a definite sense of adventure and of being on top of the world.

Santa Cruz circuit. A glacial lake

91

Our first challenge, as ever, was to negotiate the lower passes in our rickety local minibus and then agreeing terms for our donkeys, which, apparently, were so fragile that they couldn't carry three packs, only two, and needed two donkey herders and an apprentice, not just one. It wasn't long though before we were all set and we departed.

Made it to the top!

To be fair the first part of our journey did need all three locals as we negotiated a steep descent away from the road and we certainly weren't going to argue when we caught sight of a dead donkey lying abandoned at the foot of a steep ravine. The pathway soon flattened a little and then began to rise gently through a twisting valley above a stream. On that first day we trekked past tiny communities full of smiling people, some working in the almost soil-free fields. Our first campsite was a concern. It quickly became quite crowded and the smell of cooking soon filled the air, lucky really because the adjacent wood was a carelessly used communal toilet. We thought it was cold, and it was, but the apprentice, aged about nine, spent the night curled up next to a rock.

Next morning he and the second donkey man had gone and we continued our slow climb up towards Punta Union. The air was beautifully clear though hard to fill your lungs with and the different

The view from Punta Union

levels of fitness soon began to tell. Still, we were making good progress and only being passed by the super sized Swedish blokes who got up later, trekked twice as fast and were happily sipping a cold beer when we dragged our way in to the next camp.

Nevertheless, in various states of distress, we all made it to the top and were rewarded with a view that would have taken our breath away, if we had any left. The glacial valley complete with a sky blue lake stretched away beneath us and to our right Alpamayo, the Paramount Picture Mountain itself, soared majestically.

We enjoyed the moment of being higher than any of us had ever been before beginning our pained descent. I had forgotten how much it could hurt to come down off these high places. Each step was literally agony. Hot pins in each knee joint reminded me of my foolishness but it was worth it, at least I think so now. One of the boys couldn't complete the trek on foot and so one of the donkeys had to be unloaded and his pack shared between us, although our super fit and amiable guide carried most of it, most of the time.

That evening we were still above thirteen thousand feet in what must be one of the world's most beautiful valleys. We bought a few bottles from the little stall and tied string around the necks to rest them in the icy stream. They were much needed and well earned. As the sun set behind the steep cliffs you could see the frost forming

Santa Cruz circuit, Peru

in the shadow and we all rushed in to our tents to don our thermals and a few more layers and, thus protected, we enjoyed the play of light on the rocks and peaks and, as the sun went down, a full moon rose and a condor circled high over our heads. The moving shadows brought faces to life on the peaks above us and you could see where the Inca found their gods.

Next morning the group set off on a side trek up to the base camp of Alpamayo where there was meant to be a glorious view. I wouldn't have been surprised if some enterprising local hadn't set up a frame so that you could have your photo taken, but apparently not. I never personally found out because I, for the first time, decided not to make that trek, mindful of how much more of Peru lay in front of us and how much pain I'd been in the day before. Fortunately we needed a volunteer to stay and look after the kit in this busy transit

Santa Cruz. Donkeys claiming the path

Paramount Mountain

camp so my decision worked all ways.

The next phase took us past a brilliant blue glacial lake and high cliffs as we slowly made our way down the steep long path towards Cachapampas, thankful of the advice we had received from Louis, our favourite local cafe owner, to go this way round and not the other.

At the end, as we emerged from a narrow gorge weary but triumphant, we were met by a line of taxis whose business was rescuing travellers like ourselves from the last few tedious miles into town. It's one of the ironies of these "wilderness" treks that civilisation is rarely more than a stone's throw away.

Back to Huaraz for a welcome rest and a hot bath and then it was straight to the station for the bus to Chiclayo, four hundred kilometres away across the northern deserts. That was a long ride on a very basic bus, passing through Chimbote and Trujillo, both temptingly close to the cool ocean, but we pressed on, intrigued by the possibilities of the Tomb of the Lord of Sipan and the Witch Doctors Market, which between them, had put Chiclayo on the trekking map. The deserts did shimmer as the heat built and mirages created the illusion of water in the middle distance as we rattled noisily on, drowsy with heat and drifting in and out of wakefulness. Eventually that part of our journey was over and we pulled in to the station after dark. A gaggle of tuc-tucs descended upon us and the leader of the day eventually negotiated a deal and we set off towards the town to check into a reasonably comfortable hotel in time to find food in an inexpensive coy free café.

In my usual fashion I wandered off, this time accompanied by some of the students who were now getting the idea, the idea being that when you are only going to be in a place once in your life you really should make the most of it. To my surprise, and in some ways disappointment, we found yet another internet café and I began to wonder how far we had to go to be truly in the wild. We were going to find out, but not for a week or two. At that point I gave in to temptation, again, and e-mailed my wife and family to update them on our adventures so far.

Next morning, after breakfast from a street stall, we set off for the

Sipan mud temples, Deserts of Northern Peru

gravesite. The Tomb complex in fact has three burials and they are quite eerie places. Still then under excavation the cluster of skeletons in the grave of the Lord of Sipan himself, with the accompanying grave goods, mostly of beaten gold, showed that this was the last resting place of a rich and powerful man. I hope the women and child had died natural deaths and were not placed there to serve him in the afterlife. Above the tomb, in a niche, was the grave of another male, probably a guard, and I cannot think that his death was so convenient. Perhaps they regarded it as an honour and a guarantee of privilege in the next world. It has been known.

The place was dusty, desolate and very hot and we soon left in search of cold refreshment and a discussion of the ethics of putting the remains of the long dead on display. I don't suppose this Lord or his entourage would have been best pleased, although some would argue, if the earthly remains are important to a continued time in paradise, that they couldn't be safer than in the humidity-controlled sealed safety of the British Museum or their equivalent.

The local bus eventually turned up to return us to Chiclayo where

The Lord of Sipan Grave site. Northern Peru

we made our way to the Mercado Modelo, in a corner of which the Witch Doctors Market was to be found. En route we picked up a couple of young policemen who trailed us at a respectable distance, possibly just curious, or perhaps this part of town was not as safe as we thought. We had certainly achieved one of our objectives now and saw no other tourists for days.

The market was a funny old place. Not just a collection of stalls selling unrecognizable fruits and herbs but also somewhere you could go for treatment and be prescribed all sorts of exotic medications, including those made from hallucinogenic cacti. We declined all offers and contented ourselves with the purchase of lucky charms and amulets at prices that we thought were reasonable and seemed to make them happy also, always a happy balance. Haggling is OK to an extent but when you are dealing with people who are, by your standards, already very poor, why push it?

Now it was time to head up in to the mountains to begin our exploration of the Amazon itself and so we boarded yet another bus and set off for the mountain city of Chachapoyas.

Who would have thought we'd have fallen for something like that?

To really appreciate this story you have to realise just how confident we all were about being in the far-flung corners of the world.

Between the four adults in the group we had been to Alaska, Borneo, North Africa, Patagonia, New Zealand, China and who knows where else. These were the places we'd discussed over a drink in some Peruvian cafe or other. Been there, done that, and all that sort of stuff.

Now we were in Chachapoyas, a town of around twenty thousand people at seven thousand five hundred feet in the foothills of the Andes in Northern Peru and we were looking for a meal, cheap.

In Chachapoyas the owners stand outside their restaurants and tout their menus, so we were used to being politely harassed. This town, more than most we had already visited, felt like being in Northern Spain, and perhaps this put us off our guard.... there has to be some excuse for what was about to happen.

We'd been walking around enjoying the bustle of the early evening. One or the other of us had discounted all sorts of places. We were looking for something interesting with a sense of being Peruvian and so eventually we found ourselves outside the ideal place, a Mexican restaurant with a TV and plastic tables. Cheap and clean, it looked like what we needed, and yes, outside, was a little Peruvian guy in a cheap pullover with a standard Chachapoyas short back and sides in grey.

We went in, he went in. We stood around and he helped the waitresses group the tables into an uncomfortable assortment of place settings.

We sat and chatted and he went around with the waitress helping her take the order in a funny guttural mix of Spanish, English and a local language that I really couldn't get any of at all.

We ate, pizza {not very Peruvian but at least it began with a "P"} and drank our Pepsi whilst he sat, arms folded at the bar and watched in case we needed more drinks. We did, he brought them over and a pleasant meal ensued.

We chatted as he changed the channels on the TV. All the young travellers, except the student treasurer, went back to the hotel with one of the adults, whilst we finished off and swopped a few more travellers' tales, unaware that we were about to be in one.

We ordered the bill and he brought it, on a little "silver" tray.

He asked me if I'd be paying in Dollars or Sol. "Sol" I said.

He presented the bill, I paid the bill. He put the tray on the bar, the money in his pocket, and exited, stage left, pursued only by our curious gazes.

We conjectured, he fled. We drank, he ran. We assumed he'd gone to buy some more supplies or visit the local Casino … and then we tried to leave.

As we stood to go, the young waitress bought over the little "silver" tray and said, in Spanish, "You pay now please". I replied, sort of in Spanish, "We have already paid, we paid the man who served us".

"But he is not with the restaurant, we do not know him."

Far from home we thought we were being stitched up, being made to pay twice, and we were affronted that such experienced travellers could be treated in such a way, and so a "dialogue" began. Things were getting heated and loud and so, eventually, we sat down and demanded that they call the police. They didn't want to, but we insisted, and eventually a call was made.

Did the police arrive? No. Their dumpy little female lawyer arrived with her even smaller assistant and her two slightly larger male "Heavies" {Peruvians on the whole are very small and it felt like being threatened by a couple of Hobbits.}

Annoyingly, at this point, they locked the door of the restaurant and our guide became cross. We all did in our own ways.

No progress was being made and I demanded to see a uniformed policeman. They were very hesitant and reluctant but, in the end, they made another call and this time a very big man turned up in a flak jacket and carrying a gun. It says a lot, I think, that no crowd gathered outside, even though tourists were rare in that town.

I explained to him the problem, using a combination of Spanish and melodramatic acting, playing all the parts myself. He understood and began to berate the waitresses for allowing the con to succeed. They pleaded that he had told them he had been sent by the hotel to help the gringos and they hadn't thought any more about it; after all, he had entered with us and helped out, exactly why we thought he was with them. Clever.

Now we decided that enough really was enough, they were only young girls and we were only talking about thirty pounds so we decided to pay again and claim it on the insurance. Mistake.

The restaurant ladies were happy. The little lawyer was happy, the hobbity heavies were happy. Hands were shaken and tears mopped up but the unsmiling policeman insisted on being helpful. He wanted us to go to the station to fill in a form so that the insurance would pay. We tried to say "no" but that just didn't work, he was insistent, and we realised there was no way out of the inevitable form filling to come.

So, we got in to the back of the big, black 4x4 with all the guns and grenades and mace sprays and stuff, separated from us by the heavy grill, and drove slowly to the block house.

This was a two storey building built around a square courtyard, lit only from the windows. There was only one way in or out and that was a long narrow corridor with narrow slits in the walls either side. All the windows were heavily grilled. It felt like being in a spaghetti western set at the Alamo and was clearly built for defence.

We all sat at a long old school bench leaning against one wall of the inner courtyard, whilst our friendly cop wrote a report, three times, by hand, for which he needed to know our marital status, how many children we had, how long we'd been in Peru, my shoe size {well, maybe not that but it all felt a bit like that.} My attention wandered over to the far wall, which was peppered with small holes at head and chest height. I nudged our guide, and we both became even more polite than we had been before. I don't know how long those bullet holes had been there and I certainly wasn't going to ask.

Eventually, in the early hours, with all forms duly completed, stamped and distributed, we were done and the policeman insisted on driving us the two blocks to the hotel. Once outside we could see why. The streets were full of young partying Peruvians and we didn't see any other tourists at all. The crowds parted before the car without pause or question and soon we were back. The policeman shook our hands, ushered us in to the hotel and disappeared in to the night.

We'd been given our instructions for the following morning so, after a hearty breakfast of coffee and croissants {when would we find somewhere truly remote?} we set off for the bank to claim our insurance thing, or something, we weren't quite sure what.

When we got there the bank was another building built for defence with only one door and a wire perimeter fence at least twelve feet high. An armed guard policed the sole gate and two more patrolled the long, patient queue to ensure good order was maintained, no queue jumping here, or so we thought. We joined the back resigned to a long session of people watching, which wasn't such a bad thing. Within seconds though we were approached by another little, leather overcoat clad lady who offered us a place further up the queue, for a Sol.

Her business, it seemed, was to employ young boys to queue for her and then to sell their places in the queue to people at the back, brilliant. We spent our Sol and exchanged places with a smiling boy who presumably would now get some commission. This got us as far as the gate and no one seemed to have any issue with the manoeuvre.

The line snaked into the air-conditioned bank and we, eventually, were summoned to a counter. The clerk took our docket and fed the details into the computer. He smilingly {they smile a lot in Peru} asked us for four dollars, cash. We paid him, only to be handed a piece of paper that said, "You have been robbed", stamped, officially, three times, in red.

Now we joined in the smiling because we couldn't decide which robbery was the most elegant, the bandits or the banks.

I don't know whether our guide ever bothered to claim the thirty pounds.

Chachapoyas became our base for several days as the project that year, unusually, just didn't work out. This gave us time to explore a place that had become a major target during our research phase, Kuelap.

We had decided early on to avoid the south of Peru, having heard stories of the commercialisation of the Inca trail, but we were keen to explore the history of the pre-Columbians and the Inca. Kuelap, the unknown cousin of Machu Picchu, gave us just that opportunity.

The ruins here date from between the sixth to the sixteenth century and are composed of more than four hundred building remains enclosed by a massive stone battlement. At six hundred metres long, and one hundred and ten metres wide, it is a major site which then, was largely unvisited.

We set off in the usual crowded minivan that we had hired for the day, complete with driver of course. The journey took us ever higher into the remote mountains on ever more worrying roads. At times the drops were major and we wondered what would happen if something came the other way. Eventually we arrived in the Utcubamba Valley and began our ascent through the cloud forests, so called because of the wreaths of mist that drift between the dripping trees, adorned with fiery red orchids that hang surreally from the branches. Our road took us eventually to a car park, or at least an area of flat land on which we could park. The rest of the approach would have to be on foot and we set off to complete the last steep two hundred metres of our expedition. Kuelap itself is at three thousand metres above sea level so we were feeling the altitude. The approach

Entrance to Kuelap

was made more special by the roaming herd of wild Llamas that took no interest in us at all, but just munched away at the tough grass. Inevitably there was a man with a book of tickets but he did seem pleasantly surprised to see us and, after the relevant small amount of money had changed hands, he guided us to the narrow winding entrance through the massive bulwarks. We climbed up over the massive stones and found ourselves alone in a long abandoned city in the clouds. The party broke up and we all began to just wander about. There were no defined paths and clambering about made us feel like real explorers. The blood orchids {my name only I think} did seem to light the place although I'm sure that was an illusion caused by the mingling of sun, mist and canopy. There were helpful signs dotted about, one of which described the use of an inverted stone bowl several metres across, a masterpiece of

Llamas outside the walls of Kuelap

engineering, which apparently was the site of many a ritual sacrifice where prisoners were thrown in with jaguars.

At the highest end, as the clouds cleared, the views were stunning enough to make you forget that there were no railings and the vertical drop was hundreds of feet. Pulling back we crawled forward and lay a while taking it all in.

In true explorer style one of the students pulled a lose stone out of a wall to reveal a small chamber packed with bones, possibly the remains of one of those sacrificial victims but hopefully not, we couldn't see enough to determine if they were human or not and we certainly weren't going to disturb them.

We ate our lunch enjoying the solitude and then set off back to town to pack and catch the night bus to Tarapoto when we would finally be in the Amazon proper. That journey was a worry, starting at the bus station where there was a prominently displayed sign asking anyone carrying a gun to declare it to the driver. With our packs in the hold and our bags in the roof racks we set off through the night, passing now over the roof of the world. It was another long one with one moment of actual real panic when the bus negotiated a rocky river that was running across the road and hit a hidden pothole that made it swing so violently to the right that all the bags came flying off the racks to bounce off our heads. That time there were real screams and the locals looked genuinely shocked, which is the time to worry. Nevertheless we all just picked ourselves up, repacked the racks and carried on. The bus driver didn't even bother to stop.

Next morning we pulled in to Tarapoto to discover that we had several hours to wait for the next available bus to the boarding point at Yurimaguas, another night journey away, so we visited a market to buy our string hammocks and then decided to make something of the day and go white water rafting.

Flaming blood Orchids" Kuelap Cloud Forest

There were many agents about who could help make this happen and we were soon standing on the bank of a wide fast flowing river with lots of rocks. We'd never done this before but we were determined and so we donned our crash helmets and flotation jackets and got aboard the inflatable, only a little perturbed by the advice that when, note when, you fell out of the boat you should do your best to keep your feet pointing downstream so that you could fend yourself off the rocks. I asked what I thought was a fair question about what creatures we might encounter IF we did fall in. The reply was WHEN you do; you would encounter nothing because the current is too fast flowing. He didn't go on to reassure me about the possible denizens of the languid pool at the bottom of the run but then, if they were prepared to do it, so were we.

Six to a boat, braced as best we could on the inflatable cross bars, we pushed out into the increasingly rough water. Waves that had

The Sacrificial Bowl. Kuelap, Northern Peru

looked like ripples from the safety of the shore now surged around us and even above us. Black rocks were distorted beneath the fast flowing current and we were off.

Keeping the nose downstream presented a real challenge as we bounced and struggled to make some sort of use of the paddles, I wouldn't glorify what we were doing with the term "rowing". At the first serious run the first of the kids was bounced unceremoniously out of the boat with a squeal and instructions were shouted by many about heads and feet and rocks but it was all smiles as it became clear, as the second kid bounced, that this was actually what was meant to happen, but not to me. I don't like swimming and I don't like sharing my space with river monsters, even quite cute small ones, and I was determined to stay in that boat. I laced one foot around a rope and pushed the other under the inflatable crosspiece on which I was sitting and just held on. The oar was gone, lunch was gone, everyone else was happily bobbing feet first down the river and I was alone in my randomly spinning bronco of a boat. It was hilarious.

It was only a few more moments of back twisting amusement and we all arrived, one way or another, in to the swirling pool of murky water whose denizens, and I'm sure there were some, were thankfully uninterested in this offering.

105

This little bit of "rest and recreation" over we were soon on the bus and heading for Yurimaguas. The road was rough but the journey uneventful and we arrived just after dawn at this jungle town. Getting berths was easily achieved in a narrow cargo boat that was due to set off soon. This was actually a sixty-five feet long canoe with a low rigid fixed canopy and no deck. The bottom was

Amazon dug outs. NB. This photo was taken in the reserve mentioned below

filled up with sacks of produce and supplies almost to the gunwales and then we were invited to string our hammocks from side to side, making the boat about eight feet wide. Once we, the privileged first class passengers, were settled, the locals loaded up their children and themselves. The crew stoked up the open kitchen on the roof, ropes were un-slung and we drifted out in to the upper reaches of the Amazon.

That first sun set across the Andes from the river was the most magical. I quickly gave up my hammock to a grateful mother who looked like her need was greater than mine and sat with one elbow on the wooden side watching the colours playing on the water. The kids took various degrees of interest, some in their surroundings and some only in each other. As night fell we were joined for a while by a pod of pink Amazonian river dolphins that swam beside us in silent communion, setting the tone, as it turned out, for an unforgettable series of encounters in the week ahead.

The enveloping darkness was made even darker by the brightness of the Amazonian star-scape, undimmed by man-made light, and the only sound was the river passing by as the boat made its silent way between the black masses of the banks. I don't know if I slept but I do remember being surprised by the sunrise and the changing greens of the jungle. On it rolled until a settlement hove in to view and we soon arrived at Lagunas where we were met by an elderly gentleman who conducted us to the finest building in town, a wooden built villa raised on thick posts. Two rooms and, in one, two beds each with its own mosquito net. Luxury. One for me and one for my colleague Dave, I don't recall how we came to that decision but I do know that sleeping in that bed felt really good. Having settled in we walked back into town in search of food and a cold drink. We had finally arrived in a town with no internet café and we were so pleased. We sat on an open terrace, or perhaps it is better described as a room with the front wall missing, ate a simple hot meal and drank a cold beer. Later, chatting to the locals and playing cards with the kids, the lights suddenly clicked off. No one amongst the crowd reacted and it was soon explained to us that at this time each night

Travelling in style

the generator for the village was turned off and the night closed in. Undeterred we turned on our head torches and the guys brought out some oil lamps and more drinks appeared. What happened next was reminiscent of a bad horror movie as giant moths, well moths the size of my open hand which is pretty giant, came Kamikazi-ing out of the night and slammed in to our faces. Our first reaction was startled panic, brushing frantically to get them off, whilst the old guys laughed. Perhaps, on reflection, we were set up to provide a bit of light relief. Once we'd calmed down they demonstrated the accepted solution, which was to let them land wherever then grab them firmly and smash them to the floor, which was soon carpeted. I'm not suggesting this was right but it was real.

Next morning a donkey cart appeared to carry our packs and we began our trek in to the Pacaya Samiria natural sanctuary, a wildlife wonderland. The walk was easy going through flat agricultural land with our guide trotting amiably alongside. After a few kilometres the path closed in and we were wandering down a well-trodden jungle trail. At one point I stopped and asked the guide what the six foot long web funnel suspended in the bushes to the left of us was all about. He responded by slashing it open with his machete to reveal tens of thousands of miniature tarantulas scurrying for cover. It was a vast nest. We all crowded round, but not too close, and one of the kids asked where the mother was. There, he said, and there she was, sitting on a big leaf, bigly. We jumped back in case she jumped forward and ticked off our first tarantula encounter, the first of many, they were everywhere.

Hours later we arrived at the banks of a small, deep stream. It was obviously a well-established jumping off point with a small building and a strong wooden jetty and we were soon organised into a series of dugout canoes. Our packs were for resting on and we sat on wooden slats which kept us just above the water that slopped in each time the powerful wiry native Amazonian in front turned the canoe with his single paddle to navigate us through the maze of mangrove trees. It was a time to relax and enjoy and some of the kids were actually asleep by the time we were deep in to the Reserve. Our guides were clearly expert and determined to give us a good time. On cue they rowed us in to the bank after spotting something. Pointing and smiling, they directed our gaze to a large green lizard sitting on a branch above us. An Amazonian tree runner they said but I don't know if that's the right name. It was, though, about thirty centimetres long and quite agitated. It became even more agitated when the lead guide got out of his boat and began to vigorously shake the tree. I drew back and gripped hard to the sides of the canoe and then it jumped straight at me, or so it seemed. All these years later I can still see the outstretched claws which my subconscious told me were aiming for my face. In fact, of course, it was diving into the water trying to escape. It hit the surface a fraction of a second before I did, much to the amusement of all, including me, and I had inadvertently broken my promise to my wife not to get into the water. The lizards' attempt had failed and he was unceremoniously scooped out and offered up to our cameras.

On we wandered, into the warmth of the afternoon. At one point the guides excitedly leapt up and pointed fast enough for me to glimpse a stub-tailed black cat as big as a lynx cross a thick branch above and in front of us. "Taitha" they said, really energised, so I knew that we had seen something rare.

Why do I ask provocative questions? This one was "Do you think there is any chance of us seeing an Anaconda? "Anaconda? Si!" was the reply and soon we were once again jammed in to the bank in a little cluster of trepidation. The guide in my boat stood and stuck his head into a bush. He was clearly wrestling with something and, when he pulled back, literally rocking my boat, he had a metre and a half long snake twisting in his hand. "There", he said, "Anaconda" as he offered it to me to hold. I declined, sadly, just too surprised and not yet ready, and then it bit him. He calmly prised it off and threw it into the water, which convinced me that he hadn't in fact had it in a cage in the bush waiting for us.

That night we camped on a muddy bank next to a small lagoon. One tarpaulin to lie on and another stretched above us to keep off the inevitable rain, a mosquito netted plot the size of our sleeping bags each, laid out like a smorgasbord I thought, attractive to any passing man-eater. Fortunately the only man-eaters that passed were mosquitoes and they were only able to feed on those unfortunate enough to sleep with their bare arms pressed up against the nets.

Toileting was interesting involving as it did a shovel, a short walk and a tree to rest against. You have to make a decision when you are so engaged and suddenly notice a large tarantula sitting on a branch looking at you. The spider didn't seem unduly bothered and I was becoming accustomed to their company, so neither was I.

Later we were grouped around another tarpaulin having dinner. This was composed of mounds of bananas served on their own leaves and delicious fresh fish pulled from the muddy waters by our grinning guides. Having seen the creatures they were pulling from the river I had to ask why anyone would voluntarily jump in to it. Piranhas seemed to be the least of the problems. As we ate another tarantula dropped into the middle of our meal and no one flinched

from nudging it out of the way, it is odd how quickly things can be become just a part of what you do.

Night fell and we set off in our canoes in to the dark in search of caimans.

I must confess that I was more than a little nervous, particularly because there wasn't a gun in sight. I

An Anaconda in the boat.

wouldn't want any of these animals hurt but was anxious to avoid any of us becoming headlines.

The guides rowed us into narrow waterways and we scanned the banks and surface for signs of life. Our first encounter was once again sitting on a branch. A cobra … and it wasn't happy. Highlighted by the crossed beams of our head torches it reared up and spread its hood. Our cameras clicked in unison and then the same guide did the same thing, vigorously shaking the branch. The snake reared more and hissed and stared straight at me and the man was told in no uncertain terms by all of us at the same time to "STOP DOING THAT!".

On we went, the silence broken only by the quiet splash as the oars dragged us into the dark and the alarming slither and much louder splashes as some things large entered the water behind us. A branching waterway to our right was lit up by the eyes of numerous caimans picked up by our lights, presumably meaning that they were looking at us.

My guide next rammed our canoe in to a tangle of logs in the middle of a wide stretch and the boy who had been sitting behind, about twelve I think, clambered across me and acrobatically jumped on to the floating island. After briefly disappearing he reappeared with a small caiman in his hands. With a happy grin he held it out to me and, this time, I took it. Any attempt to pass it on was met with a blank stare and so I sat there enjoying the moment.

The boy had gone again, looking for other specimens I suppose,  but his return this time was much more dramatic. Jumping from branch to bobbing branch he hurled himself in to the boat and grabbed an oar. Pushing off, all the boats began paddling backwards as fast as they could. I asked what the matter was. "Tu Mama", they said, the mother. We had already worked out that the distance between the eyes indicated the size of the beast and the pair heading for us was a hands breadth apart. I realised in a moment of real fear that I was holding the

Piranha in the Amazon

baby, literally, and quickly put that right, hurling it towards the approaching croc. I didn't think caimans were particularly maternal and I may have provided it with an evening snack. Either way, I've learnt to worry when the locals do and we were out of there at speed.

After an early breakfast of ugly fish and bananas we set off for the Gran Laguna where we were told we would find VERY big snakes. We canoed a while and, as always, every journey was spectacular, this time there were monkeys everywhere careering through the canopy and sparking explosions of macaws, in dozens, whose technicolour plumage suddenly erupted from the green as the monkeys intruded. We had a discussion about collective nouns and decided that an eruption, explosion or sparkling of macaws would be appropriate. We had earlier decided, having shared many a room that a cacophony of snorers worked, so now we were just developing a theme.

We beached the canoes and, before we set off, took the opportunity to swim for the first time. The waters were so full of suspended clay that your finger vanished as you poked it in and I declined, thinking of breakfast, but the local boys jumped in and so did the students, briefly. I seemed to have achieved a sort of older man status and so was invited to sit with the head guides rather than take part in such frivolous sport and I didn't protest. Afterwards we walked a little way through the jungle. The guide invited us to climb into

Anaconda lake. El Gran Laguna

a hollow tree, which he told us was used by jaguars but was now definitely empty. Some of the party accepted and were soon briefly swallowed, but thankfully only by the tree.

When we arrived at the Gran Laguna we were met by a skeleton of a twenty-foot plus Anaconda curled up on the bank. The guide told us that birds had attacked it but we saw nothing that we thought capable of such a thing. For a long time we crouched and watched the muddy waters, not sure what to expect. We didn't see any snakes but we were able to track their movement. In three different lines small fish were jumping out of the water in piscine panic, evidence, he said of the movement of the giant Anacondas that haunted this isolated spot.

Next morning, our last in the reserve, we rose extra early and broke camp. We were careful to take everything that we had brought in and nothing else, conscious of the old adage, "leave only footprints, take only photographs."

Once loaded we set off through the early dawn heading for a dark pool of very deep water. Here we sat and waited in breathless silence. In the middle was a wooden buoy with a small bell. There was bait beneath it and it was rocked occasionally as something fed below. Our patience was rewarded when a pod of pink dolphins appeared for long enough to see but not to photograph, and then an arapaima, which the guide called a paische {apologies for the spelling}, broke the surface briefly. These 6 foot monsters are becoming increasingly rare as they are hunted for food so we were particularly pleased. The only disappointment is that we all took picture after picture of ripples and maybe, perhaps, the tip of a disappearing tail.

After this final encounter we laid back as the guides rowed us against the stream to the boarding point. It was only now that we even noticed the current and were even more impressed by the astonishing strength of these small Amazonians.

Back on land and our pockets lighter by some substantial but well-earned tips, we returned to Lagunas ready to catch the boat down to Iquitos but now, for the first time, things did not go smoothly. We donned our packs and moved down to the river. Access to the boats was via a dozen or so roughly cut steps in a slippery mud bank and beneath them was the swirling water of the big river. As the first boat came in through the darkness we all became increasingly anxious. One by one we made our way down the treacherous steps and on to the boat, but now, the leader of the day, decided that this boat was not for us. Being as it was, too hot and smelly and so, to the amusement of all, we disembarked. This later provoked the only serious disagreement we had on any expedition, albeit briefly, and meant that we had to spend another two days in this small town before we could get another boat. At least it gave us a chance to begin to appreciate what life was like here by exploring independently the streets and shops and enjoying the hospitality of the locals, with whom we could only communicate by smiling. It also allowed us to swim and some did, enjoying the attention of the small piranha that nipped playfully at them. We were told they were too small and well fed by dropping fruit to be a danger, and so it turned out since all emerged with no more than a scattering of small red marks of honour.

Eventually a much bigger boat docked which did give us a more comfortable and interesting journey down the river. This one had three decks and we were on top on the tourist and / or first class local traveller deck. Here we had room to string our hammocks and walk around and there was a small dining room, a luggage room with two beds, where Dave and I actually slept, and access to cold drinks.

Below us was the more crowded but still quite nice second class deck, still with hammocks but without hot food, and below that was

Tuc-Tucs in Iquitos

the cattle deck where people bedded down between the livestock, close to the river and the engines.

Time did drift by like the now immense river and I genuinely have no idea how long we spent on that boat. I remember a fabulous sunset behind us on one evening and a spectacular rainstorm with an accompanying cold wind on another, areas of bank collapsing in to the water where the trees had been cleared, tiny jungle villages where the children ran waving along the paths and a confluence with a dark tributary, whose chocolaty waters carried islands of blossom in to the lighter waters of our river, swirling like coffee and cream.

The Rio Maranon on which we were travelling merged first with the Rio Tigre and then the Rio Ucayali to become the Rio Amazon and a lifelong ambition was achieved. Soon we would be docking in Iquitos, approachable only by air or water and the end of our outward journey.

As we approached the complex of jetties, different groups beneath us got to work. Fast skiffs raced alongside and young men began to leap into our boat to collect the crop of bananas for the morning market, throwing the huge bunches back and then leaping across without any sign of hesitation or concern after which, with a friendly wave, they sped away. Now the front of our boat became the focus as the crew began to haul in the long chains that they had dropped over the previous evening. On the end were the biggest

The Iron House, Iquitos

catfish I could imagine were possible. Estimating them against the men who were busy avoiding their mouths whilst dispatching them with machetes, they must have been six feet and maybe more.

The catfish sorted, a cow was now led out and as the machete was raised we collectively turned away. Presumably this was destined for a market on the fast approaching shore and was to be sold quickly and fresh.

We braved the Tuc-Tucs to reach our accommodation, the quaintly named "Hobos Hideout", just off the Plaza de Armas. Bustling and vibrant with a complex mix of peoples attracted first by the rubber boom and later by tourism, Iquitos felt good. We found that we could use the pool at the five star hotel on the square so long as we bought a few drinks and so, finally, we began to relax and take in some sun.

Later, refreshed and recharged, we explored the Belen district with the largest ethnic market in the Amazon where all major cards were accepted and where one hopeful stall holder asked Dave if he could borrow a few coins off his Dad to make the price she wanted, meaning me. When we had stopped laughing we calculated that I was in fact old enough to fill that role, so the lady was forgiven and I was depressed.

Gifts purchased, in my case a set of amazonite jewellery, we wandered the muddy streets between stilt houses and came across a school. Rows of children sitting in a dark windowless room with not one book in sight. I tried to explain that I was a teacher with the intention of letting them ask us questions and asking them some of our own but the language barrier was just too big and we all smilingly gave up.

Cat fish. Pulled out of water in the Amazon
that they expected us to swim in.

Later we adjourned to The Iron House on the main square. This prefabricated iron clad iconic building has stood there since 1890, a relic of the rubber boom. Designed by Gustav Eiffel, it is now a club with a restaurant with an international menu and I took great delight in eating a peppered steak one night and an excellent Beef Stroganoff the other, both under the brooding presence of an Anaconda skin stretched along the wall which must be close on thirty foot. I'm glad all we saw at the Gran Lagunas was panicking fish and not the reason for their acrobatics.

Our Peruvian adventure was now drawing to a close and after another long wait, we boarded our flight. It took a few hours to get us back to Lima where we bought expensive souvenirs, most of which are still in the box, and watched people hang gliding above major roads and crowded parks before making our way to the airport for the long flight home.

Chapter 10 - Travelling with children in the UK

London

It would be just wrong to devote all of our attention to taking children abroad when we have one of the world's great cities practically on our doorstep. Visits with children have taken many guises. Amongst them there have been history trips of various sorts and adventures taking children to auditions for various films and shows, or for the National Youth or National Youth Music Theatres. Visits to West End shows, museums and monuments or just for fun are also popular. They have all produced entertaining tales over the years.

So, auditions. These are in most cases a cruel business. Children full of hope and aspiration are herded into basic rooms in often-dingy areas to interminably wait their turn. In some they get half an hour in a group, in others four minutes of solo performance, mostly ending with rejection. To soften this harsh process I usually managed to build in a visit to a show, although these days the prices in the West End have made that prohibitive, and, of course, lunch.

When Planet Hollywood first opened just off Leicester Square it was a great place to take kids, or even just to eat if you're into movies. The steak was actually very good. I happened to be there once when they were offering a Planet Hollywood credit card so I took one out and have it still. The main advantage of this was that it gained you privileged access and I used to really hope there would be a queue outside the door and an hour's wait for a table, because flashing the card meant the rope was lifted and you were straight in. I know this conflicts with my views about fast tracks and theme parks mentioned later but I'm weak and I just couldn't help it. The various young travellers over the years were always very impressed by this film star treatment, which made up for the drab audition spaces.

One time when we were there, the waiters were all dressed in particularly wild and colourful shirts. I asked politely if it was possible to buy one and was told, sadly, no. I asked the waiter to check with the manager and he did, and came back and the answer was still no. I let an hour pass as we ate our meal and then called him over again and suggested he might like to go and tell the manager that Mr De Niro was in the restaurant and had expressed an interest in having a shirt. Seconds later the said manager came bursting through the kitchen doors with a gift-wrapped shirt in hand. He skidded to a halt as he realised the truth, fortunately he saw the funny side and I have that shirt still. It doesn't fit, but hey ho.

It may have been the same time but was certainly the same era when we had just paid our bill and one of the boys was heading for the loo when there was a commotion in the entrance and a group of men in dark glasses and suits entered, clearly the entourage of someone since this was in the days when celebrities still dined there. It took only a moment to spot the towering shape of Frank Bruno, head and shoulders above the big men who were there to protect him from foolish chancers. By some fluke the thirteen year old strolled through the surrounding heavies and walked straight in to the world champion. It was a comic moment as he looked up and up and Mr Bruno starred benignly down. He was a model of courtesy and grace and clearly amused by the close encounter.

No visit to London for whatever reason was ever complete without an encounter with large marine creatures. My favourite for years was a visit to the Natural History Museum. After we had got past the, "oh this was in that movie" section of the day I would lead the way through the remarkable displays of stuffed animals into the Whale Hall. If you are looking for wow moments with kids you really would have to try hard to do better than this. The first view of a full sized model of a blue whale suspended from the roof is truly awesome. The largest creature ever to grace the planet, even walking round it counts as exercise and there is always a moment when I'm there when I think about the encounters in Alaska. I know humpbacks aren't anything like as big, as the suspended skeletons prove, but big enough to provide a true adventure.

Once, when leaving the museum, some of the kids expressed a wish to visit Harrods so we walked in what I thought was the correct general direction. After a little while I began to get sniping comments and hard stares, these children had travelled with me before, and so I decided to hail a cab. It was only a short while before one pulled over and we all got in. "Harrods Please". I said. The driver glanced in the mirror, put the cab in gear, did a swift U turn across the road and stopped. "Here you are, Sir," he said. A moment of silence was followed by howls of laughter, mostly from me. It was nice that, in the spirit of London Cabbies, he had never turned the meter on and just enjoyed the joke.

More recently our travels have included the amazing shark tank at the London Aquarium in the old Greater London Council Buildings. Stretching up two storeys and viewable from every angle, including now from above through a glass bridge, this huge tank contains any number of these lethargic prehistoric monsters whose teeth seem to graze the glass as they swim endlessly around the Easter Island Head in the centre. Fascination is a sign of successful engagement in children and this display provides that in bucket loads, but if you really want to impress then make sure that you are there at feeding time. As the offerings are dropped in, the nonchalant lethargy is replaced by a frenzied, boiling turmoil that you would very much not want to be a part of. I wish I'd seen that before I decided that it was OK to swim in the South China Sea…..

Archaeological Expeditions

In the eighties I was employed to teach Archaeology as well as History and the college ran an excavation of a Romano-British iron-making site on the Weald. On the back of this, and with a small dedicated group, I ran two weeklong expeditions in the UK to explore the more spectacular archaeological destinations. One of these was to Wiltshire and the other to South Wales.

We camped on both, the first in a field lent to us by a friendly farmer and the other in a Deer Park surrounding Margam Abbey.

In Wiltshire there is a wealth of monuments, Stonehenge being the most famous, but we focused our visit on the complex around Avebury, which I think is by far the more impressive, if only because you can still get in amongst the stones {and in the case of some of the teenage archaeologists, on top of them} and get some sense of their significance to those who built them. We bought some divining rods and a number of the boys could make them spin like helicopter blades as they approached the points where stones had once stood.

One of them developed a hypothesis about Silbury Hill. He decided that the only reason to build something so big, in the absence of a grave, was as a vantage point to link all the monuments and burials together. He expected to be able to see some immense pattern and to be able to join the dots into a secret message from the pre-ancient world. Inevitably this meant we had to climb it and so, before dawn one day, we did. There was a fairly well trodden path so we didn't feel too guilty and we all waited with baited breath for the sun to come up. It did and long shadows stretched across the quiet world, touching one stone after another and revealing…. nothing. At least not to us but the idea was interesting.

Next day we drove into Bath in the minibus. This beautiful ancient city is full of historic wonders but then at least, was a nightmare for parking. Having given up on the streets we headed for an underground facility. There was of course a height limit but I thought we would be OK, we weren't. As I edged in one of the boys stood in front to watch the roof. Unfortunately he wasn't very tall and the back of the bus was higher than the front and, inevitably, we crunched in to the RSJ and got stuck. After the "Sorry Sir" and "Not to worry" conversation we had the brilliant idea of letting down the rear tyres so that the bus would be freed. Our plan worked and we drove confidently in and parked. Fortunately we had a foot pump so we took it in turns to re-inflate the tyres and went off to enjoy our visit.

When we got back we all got in and confidently drove towards the exit which was the same as the entrance and….oops, not our brightest moment.

Wales was different. There is, of course, prehistoric settlement there but we focused on the industrial and drove up the decaying Rhonda and down the heads of the valley road to Neath and then back down the M4 to junction 37 to go and sit outside The Angel Inn at Kenfig which then had a view which, to me, summed up Wales.

The fabulous natural beauty of the Gower Peninsula and Swansea Bay to the left, across the rolling dunes of Kenfig with its tiny castle, then Swansea across the bay, swinging around to the refineries of Neath and the immense steelworks at Port Talbot, crossing the M4 to look at Margam Abbey nestling in the hills and then the mountains rising up to Brecon beyond. All the elements of a Welsh landscape are there and we returned many times in that week.

Travelling with very small children

One of our feeder primaries used to run a short trip to York every year for year six. This was a considerable enterprise involving trains to London Victoria, tubes across to St Pancras and then the long run up country.

Even though these children were only weeks away from joining my school they seemed very small and I often ended up carrying several over-packed bags.

Highlights of this tour included a river trip and a visit to the National Rail Museum and the nice thing is that, aged just eleven, all of them were still at that wide-eyed age where pretty much everything was new and every experience had a "wow" moment. The most "wowie" being the train to Scarborough {I think.}

I'd heard of this so I took a little trip to the station to reconnoitre and found, to my delight, that I had heard right. The train from York to Scarborough was in fact the real Hogwarts Express!

Inevitably we had to do it, and so tickets were duly bought and the children brought down, not knowing. Led on to the platform with their eyes closed there was a huge collective gasp as they opened their eyes and took in what was happening. When they realised that they were actually going on it they moved from wow to wonderland and the whole journey was spent taking it in turns to sit in the actual carriage. We are still convinced that the lady serving refreshments was in fact the lady from the film. We were actually pleased that you couldn't buy the magical snacks, it made it feel more real.

I did that trip four times, but that was definitely the moment.

DisneyLand and the Three Parks Challenge

Back now to the world of children taller than one point four metres for the penultimate section. Living in Sussex makes Disneyland Paris easily achievable and we have been there virtually every year since it's been open, sometimes with more than a hundred children at a time. It is the most magical of places and even though its rides {except Space Mountain and The Rocking Roller Coaster} are sometimes over shadowed these days, you can't get away, in my view, from the sheer magic and showmanship of Disney. Everything is thought through and you are Disney-fied until you drop.

I loved a moment on our first trip when one cool thirteen year old caught sight of a certain mouse and shouted, "It's Mickey!" before running across for a big hug.

The music follows you everywhere leading you to that monument to both the best and the worst of Americana, "It's a Small World". Round you go, slowly, as that song repeats and repeats and the same grinning face grimaces at you from a thousand automated mannequins in dozens of different national costumes and, just when you think it really can't get any worse, they take you round one more corner and ambush you with a glittering version of Hollywood. I actually quite like it and I must confess to conning any number of kids into getting on it with tales of mega drops and watery loops......

But when you've run around all day and done all the great show piece rides too numerous to list, and as the crowds thin, there is only one way to finish the day and that is by getting the whole group on Space Mountain as many times as possible. On a good day you can easily get into double figures and we've had claims of twenty plus. I've managed sixteen in a day but, of course, hold the record because I go back every year and the children rarely go more than twice.

Our record breaker took place in the year that the college decided to have three activity days at the end of the summer term. I was part of the planning team and my contribution was to set up visits to Alton Towers, Thorpe Park, and Disneyland on consecutive days. "Sadly" our staffing was a bit stretched and we couldn't find three leaders with the right experience so...I decided to lead all three.

Day one Alton Towers, returning by midnight.

Day two Thorpe Park, back home by 8pm.

Day three Disneyland, leaving at 11pm on day two and in the park by 9.30am on day three. Fantastic.

We initially limited the children to a maximum of two parks each but as it worked out there was a posse that got to do all three with me.

On the way to Alton Towers one of my colleagues actually managed to leave a child in the loo at a service station, but only briefly. The visit itself for me was made memorable by the two very anxious year sevens who sort of wanted to get on Oblivion but were enjoying being frightened by the prospect. Eventually I convinced them to join me and we began to queue. As we got nearer the front they became more and more apprehensive and I thought they might step through and run for it but no, they were brave and strapped themselves in.

For those who don't know, Oblivion is an extreme ride that takes you slowly up a very long rise in a carriage several seats across but only two rows deep, with the back row raised so there is no escaping the sight of the monstrous drop into the steam filled black hole at the bottom of the seemingly vertical ninety foot cliff that they fire you down. To make sure you get the full impact they hold you at the top just long enough to make you wish you were somewhere else and then, bang.

On this occasion we got to just a fraction before that point and the mechanism jammed and we sat and we sat and we sat some more. As time passed the kids got more and more upset and as the tears began I began to talk to the man standing alongside making the point that we really had to get these kids off. "Not to worry", he said, "It's fixed n....", and we were catapulted off, screaming, to face our doom.

Seconds later I helped the boys off the ride and was trying to calm them down, when a kind ride operative, by way of making up for their appalling experience and distress, came over and gave them a free copy each of the ride photo in which, of course, they were crying, screaming and covered in snot. I hope they still have them.

All the main rides achieved it was back to the coach for the six hour journey home and a brief night's sleep, then back on the same coach for the thankfully short trip to Thorpe Park. By now we were on a mission and we moved as one around the park ticking off each ride as we completed it, taking advantage of the fact that this was still term time and the queues were minimal. A good thing really, because the habit of selling fast track tickets to customers who can afford them, endlessly allowing them to jump any queue, generally makes me so cross I stop queuing at all.

Back home, a quick meal and a shower and we were off again. Coach to Dover, a pleasant crossing and that drudgy drive down over the Somme to Disney. Our action plan in place we headed straight for Thunder Mountain, always worth ticking off first because it's the only major rollercoaster in the park that little people can get on. Space Mountain, Star Tours and It's a Small World before pausing to reassess. Pirates of the Caribbean, long before the films came out, The Crazy Temple ride, running backwards, and off to Phantom Manor. Lunch on Main Street at 3pm to catch the parade with a window seat, and then round again. Finishing off with a Space Mountain Fest to end the day.

Must be some kind of record.

Sam on a scary ride at Disney

Chapter 11- Last Tango in Tossa

I'm actually writing this on a coach on the way to Port Aventura in the middle of the last ever tour that I will lead with children. The sun is shining, the children are settled and watching a bad movie whilst also being excited about the day ahead and this is shaping in to an archetypal tour.

Shambhala and Dragon Khan entwine at Port Aventura

Things didn't start well. Even after so many previous departures I am completely OCD about checking everything. I check everything five times and my wife then checks each of my checks. It occurred to me during double check three that something was missing. We didn't appear to have any medical consent forms. Where could they be? Had my trusty secretary let me down? No, it was me. This was the second of two tours this year to the same place, demand had been so high, and I had been handed the forms in one pile for both trips months before and so they were now carefully filed on a Saturday in an office to which I had no access. The ability to problem solve on the hoof is an essential characteristic of a party leader and so I solved the problem, or rather we did. I knocked up a swift copy and my wife spent the half hour before departure getting parents to fill them in.

Last Tango in Tossa. Late night patrolling

With everything in place, we waved our way out of the playground and we were off in our lovely new Mercedes coach. Less than thirty minutes later Jake gave his friend Bob a little present. A perfectly inverted shepherd's pie, deposited without warning in his lap, artistic. A whole kitchen roll and many wet wipes later and we were back in business heading for Stop 24 and then on to Dover.

A brief history of the Somme as we crossed the battlefield, a game trying to spot the Eiffel Tower from the Peripherique, a smooth run through the Auvergne and a round of applause as we succeeded in crossing the Millau Viaduct, which we discovered from our helpful driver is high enough to put the Canary Wharf tower underneath it, and we were almost in Spain. Three, two, one and past the sign at La Jonquera and we were almost done, which in terms of these journeys means that three hours later, we pulled up in Tossa Del Mar. Twenty two hours in the blink of an eye, honest.

What a gem of a resort Tossa is! Having been there only a few weeks before with forty three other great kids I was very relaxed and the check in, with the help of the multilingual local agent, to the Hotel Don Juan was smooth and efficient. I took the party for a short walk to the sandy raised beach in its rocky cove, topped by a fairy tale medieval castle and the holiday began. With the area of safe wandering defined and staff strategically placed, the children disappeared to begin shopping and running around.

Later we had a huge dinner in the buffet, another first for many on the trip, and one Spanish disco later it was bedtime which, after

Street Festival in Tossa. 2013

A 'Busker" on Las Ramblas

a twenty two hour journey, was easy. This night did though produce the one memorable overheard conversation from one of the rooms, which was, "we both have the same thing but mine's bigger than yours", which actually referred, of course, to two cans of deodorant.

Day three found us in Barcelona. The Nou Camp was relatively empty and the Ramblas relatively full. In between we visited the Olympic stadium, which was being resurfaced after an X games. The air was pungent with manure and one student commented that it smelt like England? We ignored the scaffolding-clad Sagrada Familia and, having not been robbed on the Ramblas, much to the disappointment of the children with back pockets stuffed with rubbish, we admired the mega-yachts in the harbour as we returned home.

Day four and Port Aventura was everything we had come to expect. This park is an absolute solid favourite and a place I will revisit again and again, even though there are rides that I won't get on any more, like the Hurakan Condor which is visible from miles away and the Furious Baco, a roller coaster which accelerates so fast that when I did get on it I actually thought it was broken and we were all going to die! The kids though, love it. {I'm writing this later in the week.} No queues again. Younger staff passing by with strings of kids in tow, which used to be my role, whilst I manned the check in and managed a large pile of rotating bags at the entrance to the Dragon Khan. That day I didn't even get on that and only

Spain 2010 Eric at the Olympic Stadium

managed one visit to the thrilling Templo Del Fuego before we set off happily home collecting the statistics of the day. Eight goes on Shambhala, the highest ride in Europe, took the one day title, but I think my sixty five goes on the Dragon Khan over the years will stand for a while.

That evening the dance floor was once again taken over by a large group of elderly Spaniards who objected to the children trying to do the Macarena to a waltz, then compromised by teaching the more adventurous to Tango. After the children were sent off to bed I was the only one to witness the snake cabaret, startled to walk in to see a man with a ten-foot albino python wrapped around him. Upstairs, six of the kids had taken on the role of Hall Monitors and were marching up and down with professional resolution.

Montserrat, day five, and I almost got to go on the cable car until two of the children lost their resolve and got back on the coach. Rats! Later though, I was allowed to ride the funicular to the top for the long walk back and for the first time in thirty years found the air clear enough to allow us to see the Spanish Border, Barcelona and the Balearics in the same view. Nearly all of the children went to

Tom and Jordan buying sweets in the market in Barcelona

touch the Black Madonna whilst I sat in the sunshine and then back to the Hotel.

This night the dance floor was occupied by a large group of exuberant German students, a little older than ours, who were really going for it with considerable style. Fascinated, ours began to join in and a real party broke out. By now we had given up on bedtimes since the hotel was a reverberating drum until midnight when the music abruptly stopped, the magnets released the stair doors and a sleepy silence fell.

Day six took us to the Dali museum where I was able to share the discovery of the kids on the first trip that using your phone to view the picture with the keyhole produced the face of Lincoln. They were definitely wowed, one to the extent that she began photographing everything, including a fire hydrant….

An afternoon wander in the beautiful old town of Girona produced an excellent set of photos of this last ever group and some more excellent shopping. I was pleased that the lady in the fabulous shop next to the square remembered me as the "teacher from a few weeks back with all the nice children".

Spain 2010 Montserrat Cable car close up

No Germans on the dance floor when we got back, but a parrot cabaret instead. It was really nice that this hotel, and indeed this resort, felt like the Salou of thirty years ago and was able to give the children a taste of the real Catalunya, a fitting end. Our students stepped in to the gap left by the Germans, having had the behaviour so well modelled, and happily entertained a tiny Spanish girl who was there with her family. A few of the German girls turned up for the last dance so Harry was happy, and then off to bed for one last night in a hotel with students safely tucked away off the silent corridor.

Last day and I climbed the hill towards the castle looking for a shady terrace with the best view, a preoccupation of mine, only to find that three of the kids had gotten there first and were already ordering an early lunch, well taught indeed. A large group wanted to carry on fishing, having bought rods and bait the day before so we facilitated that on the rocky promontory, with a big enough gap for lunch for the staff in a pleasant beach side restaurant whilst the fisher kids sat at a respectful distance, waiting for me to finish so they could resume their clambering searches for their elusive prey.

The coach loaded, the border crossed and another movie on the DVD player and this journey is drawing to a close. The main theme has actually just started and my days of travelling with children are almost done.

Fortunately my days of travelling with grandchildren are about to begin and who knows what adventures and stories in the making are about to unfold?

Group shot in Girona 2013

About the Author

Gareth Jones has been teaching combinations of History, Drama and Archaeology in the South East of England for over thirty years. Very early on he realised the inestimable value of travelling for children and so he has led trips all over the world to places as far-flung as Borneo, Peru and Alaska, as well as to a range of British and European destinations. As a result he has spent the equivalent of two and a half school years on trips and expeditions and accumulated the exciting and \ or amusing tales contained in this book. He thinks that this entitles him to retire early…..

Other works by Gareth Jones
Georgina and the Dragon
And
Jason and the Astronauts {Schoolplay}
The Big Activity Book for KS3 Drama {Zigzag}
Dealer's Choice, Kobo

Acknowledgements

I would like to thank my wife Beverley and my good friends Tim and Tony for proof reading my early versions of the text, and Sarah, Lucy and Alex for sharing their encouraging opinions with me.

I would also like to thank the dozens of teachers and thousands of children who have travelled with me over the years, sharing the creation of these stories and adventures.

Particularly Roger and Val, Mike and Jane, Barry and Anicq and Steve and June for their constant friendship, dedication and companionship on these trips and elsewhere.